AM I
OLD YET?

AM I
OLD YET?

THE STORY OF TWO WOMEN,

GENERATIONS APART, GROWING UP AND GROWING

YOUNG IN A TIMELESS FRIENDSHIP

LEAH KOMAIKO

St. Martin's Press
New York

Designed by Gwen Petruska Gürkan

Grateful acknowledgment is given for permission to quote from the following:
"Searching for My Love." Words and music by Bobby Moore. © 1966 Chevis Publishing Corp. BM1. Original record produced by Billy Davis.
"Always" by Irving Berlin. © copyright 1925 by Irving Berlin. © copyright renewed. International copyright secured. All rights reserved. Reprinted by permission.
"Dancing in the Dark" by Bruce Springsteen. Copyright © 1984 by Bruce Springsteen (ASCAP). Reprinted by permission.
"God Bless America" by Irving Berlin. © copyright 1938, 1929 by Irving Berlin. © copyright assigned to Winthrop Rutherfurd, Jr., Anne Phipps Sidamon-Eristoff, and Theodore R. Jackson as Trustees of the God Bless America Fund. International copyright secured. All rights reserved. Used by permission.
"I Love the Nightlife (Disco Round)." Written by Alicia Bridges and Susan Hutcheson. © 1977 Lowery Music Co., Inc.

Library of Congress Cataloging-in-Publication Data

Komaiko, Leah.
    Am I old yet? : the story of two women, generations apart, growing up and growing young in a timeless friendship / Leah Komaiko.
        p.   cm.
    ISBN 1-58238-048-1 (alk. paper)
    1. Female friendship.   I. Title.
HM1161.K66   1999
302.3'4'082—DC21   99-23977
                                                          CIP

First Edition: October 1999

10   9   8   7   6   5   4   3   2   1

For Barbara Linkevitch and Patti Breitman

Contents

Part I: A Fear of Aging

Part II: A Home for the Aging

Contents

PART III: A COMING OF AGING

PART ONE

A Fear of Aging

So Young to Be So Old

To begin with, I was not aging graciously. Not that I ever had. I remember July 16, 1969. It was about a month and a half after my birthday. I was at my boyfriend Bart Potter's house in Chicago and we were on the floor in the living room. His mother and stepfather were on the sofa. We were all watching television. Buzz Aldrin and Neal Armstrong were stepping out of Apollo 11 in their space suits. In an instant they became the first human beings in the history of the world to walk on the surface of the moon. The living room was so quiet you could hear who wasn't breathing. "That's one small step for man," Armstrong said, "one giant step for mankind." Suddenly I started to cry.

"I'm old," I wailed. "I'm seventeen!"

Even before that I had gone through a phase where I could only leave the house to go to and from school. If I saw an older woman walking in the park or pushing a cart in the grocery store, I would sob until I calmed down enough to hyperventilate. How long these jags lasted depended on how old the woman was and whether she got a good look at me, too. If we locked eyes, I could be frozen in time and in my bedroom for days. For I had seen the terrorizing

3

truth of our destinies. One day I was going to be old. No day would she ever again be young. Such was life. God was demented.

I finally reached a point of peace one night during puberty when I decided I would believe in God's goodness if He could perform two miracles. The first was to let there be the invention of a knife that could simply and safely cut fat from the human body like a "Vegematic." The second would be to let me live until I was 105 with the body and mind of a twenty-five-year-old. Thirty years later my prayers had brought me to Los Angeles, the liposuction capital of the universe. I had not had the procedure, but I also no longer wanted to live to be 100. That desire had become irrelevant because I had come to believe in eternity. There was no beginning to life. There would never be an end. Therefore, there could only be a middle and this was it. I was forty-four and in the middle and stuck there forever. I didn't know what I was supposed to do with myself.

On a day-by-day basis my life was not unlivable. I had a sweet little house, I had published eighteen books for kids, and although I was bordering on burned out, I was writing a series of "chapter books" for readers in the first through third grades and working on a project for Disney. With the exception of my mother, who had died ten years earlier, my immediate family was still alive. I had married and divorced, and although I had no children of my own, because of my books I had been with roughly a hundred thousand kids in schools across the country. I had traveled and lived in four cities. I dated men who had no police records, and I had wonderful friends all over the country. We joked about the good old days and the not-too-distant future when we would all have Alzheimer's. What we couldn't admit in that moment was that we had already forgotten who we were supposed to be.

We were the baby boomers. We were the majority. No matter

how many people came after us, we would always be the majority. We would be the hip and sagely. They would be the young and pimply. They would hang on our every word.

For we were the Beatles. We were The Beach Boys and Dylan and Aretha and Smokey Robinson. We were Janis Joplin. We were "The Boss." We buried "The King" and we touched the cape of the Godfather of Soul. We were rock and roll. We were Jimi Hendrix and Grace Slick and The Doors and the Stones. That's who we were, all right. Forever. But now suddenly we were computer geeks striving to be techno-nerds, when all that cyberspace was was the revenge of the generation that had really bad music.

I decided I had to talk this all over with some friends to make sure I wasn't the only one struggling with all this.

"Do you know how much better off this country would have been if we didn't steal all the land from the Indians?" my friend Eva asked at lunch one day. "Look at the Lakotas or the Hopi or the Ojibwas. They worship their elders. Can you imagine what it would be like to live in a culture where you could actually look forward to being old?"

Not really. We lived in L.A. This was not the place to get old. If it was, somebody would have done it already.

"Why don't you get a dog?" my friend Annie in New York asked. "It gives you something to love you unconditionally." Annie knew from experience. She got Hero and the two of them became an item. Then Barbara got a puppy named Sophie Mae.

"We're having a shower for Sophie Mae," Annie called to tell me. "All the women we know who have dogs but no kids are coming. It's the new paradigm. Can you fly out? You don't want to wait to see Sophie until her bas mitzvah, do you?"

"Why don't you take a vacation?" my friend Betsy once asked.

"Familiarity breeds contempt." I knew Betsy was right. That's why I moved or left town once every six weeks. But that was before, when I was in my early thirties and I could still sleep on anything—anywhere.

Now I was older. To sleep, I had to have a choice of heating pads (steam or dry for back pain), a night neck collar, lavender aromatherapy, valerian root, calcium magnesium and vitamin D to ward off osteoporosis, and a fan or air conditioner running twelve months a year to block out the noise from my neighbor's barking dogs. I kept a boom box by my bed so I could pop in cassettes of the sounds of rain forests, sacred harp duets, or a choir singing "Om Namaha Shivaya." I needed a flashlight, gym shoes, an extra set of car keys, bottles of water, and a can of sardines at arm's length (earthquake preparedness), and I was hard put to fall asleep without at least a half hour of *David Letterman* followed by flipping through a pile of spiritual books on my nightstand. Also, I had to have easy access to Fuji apples, as I was prone to eat one in bed before I could fall asleep at night, and an eye mask in case the sun came up too early in the morning. In short, packing had become problematic.

"Maybe it's just time to get remarried," my friend Jenny said. I had known Jenny since we were in the third grade. We grew up across the street from each other in Chicago. I listened to her before I listened to anybody. "If I were single today, I'd join a dating service," she said. "You can't expect to meet people just by meeting people. Not that there's anybody out there worth meeting."

I trusted Jenny's advice, but there was no way I was going to join a dating service and look through headshots of guys to pick out "the one." I couldn't even do that for ten minutes at the police station after I had been mugged.

"So forget about a dating service," Jenny said. "Just call a match-maker. I've heard there's somebody really good in Beverly Hills."

The matchmaker had three "clubs" I could join. In the first club, I could pay $2,500 for three months to be introduced to men who earned $100,000 a year or under. For $5,000, I'd get three months of intros to men earning between a hundred thousand and a quarter of a million. For $25,000 I could meet three months of millionaires. And for $35,000, I could be fixed up on a date with the celebrity of my choice provided he wasn't married or gay.

"You don't want to end up old and alone, do you?" the match-maker asked. She could tell just by talking to me I could be married in three months, easy. Didn't I see her on *Geraldo*? Had I ever heard of Oprah Winfrey?

I felt intense despair. I had heard my final option and it wasn't an option. An instant later a clear breeze seemed to come through my head and I heard the words, "Volunteer. Go visit someone who really is old and alone. Get over yourself. Be like a Girl Scout. You'll like it." For the first time in a long time I felt some hope.

I said good-bye to the matchmaker and the next day I called a nonprofit organization called the Elder Corps that found compan-ions for the old and lonely.

"I'd like to volunteer to be matched up," I said. "What are the re-quirements?"

"Are you breathing?" the voice on the other end asked. "We can use you."

Three days later a woman named Marilyn from the Elder Corps met me for an interview at a coffee shop. She was about five years older than me, with short, graying hair.

"I like to think of myself as a matchmaker," Marilyn said. "Do you mind if I ask you a few questions? Do you care if your adoptee is in a wheelchair? Do you prefer a man or a woman? Do you want to see someone who still lives in her home or would you mind seeing someone in a care facility?"

It's not that I had never been inside one of those places before. After college I visited my grandmother four times a week at the Darrow Plaza. The Darrow Plaza was a place where people who had to give up their homes waited to move into their plots. In the summer, patients sat outside in wheelchairs with blankets covering their laps. They kept looking to see any possible action that walked or drove by. They held little wads of Kleenex in their fists so they had something to spit into should they need it.

My grandmother rarely sat outside. She stayed in her bed with a spit pan positioned under her chin. I could hear her coughing as soon as I came through the front door. Inside and outside the Darrow Plaza were two different worlds. Outside, birds and some fresh air. Inside, the smell of damp diapers, ammonia, and medicine. Lots of medicine and the sound of the television always blaring in the Community Room.

"Hi, Mrs. Kester," I would say. Mrs. Kester was my grandmother's roommate. She sat in her chair.

"How are you today, Grandma?"

"Aggh . . . how should I be doing?"

"Do you want to go outside and sit with the other people?"

"No."

"Do you want to sit in the TV room?"

My grandmother looked at me like I was deranged. Then she rubbed a string of saliva into the side of her pan. "Those people don't ever want to watch anything good. I'm just a stranger here," she said. "A stranger in paradise."

I would sit at the end of the bed while she struggled to cough and spit. I tried to make her laugh. "Score," I'd say as the first phlegm hit the pan. "Excellent form . . . an Olympic contender."

"I don't know how to die," my grandmother would cry at the end. "I've lived my whole life and I don't know how to die."

I remembered all that now and that I seemed to make it through that okay. But that was twenty years ago when I was still young enough to believe those people could never be me. I thought I would never die. Now I knew I was going to die, I just didn't believe it would happen in this lifetime.

"I guess seeing a woman in a nursing home would be fine," I told Marilyn. "If that's where you need me."

"Well, there's about six million people in different nursing homes and senior facilities in America," Marilyn said, "and roughly half of them rarely or never have a single visitor. They have nobody. Their families put them in these places, then abandon them. The problem is no better here in Los Angeles. And it makes you think, 'What's going to happen when I'm old?' A care facility costs a lot of money. That's just for someplace decent. That's just now. Thirty years from now who knows how much it will cost. Especially for people like you who have no children of their own. You can't wait until you're sixty to start thinking about this stuff."

I nodded as if I had already started planning for my golden years, when in truth I was still secretly waiting for my genuine childhood to begin. I felt completely embarrassed because I knew Marilyn was right. I had nobody. Who was I going to have to abandon me in my old age?

"It's documented that having a friendship means more to the health of the sick and elderly than medicine," Marilyn said.

"I'm happy to help," I said.

"We ask that you commit to visiting with your adoptee one hour a week where she lives. When you travel, drop the person a postcard or call. Otherwise the person might get confused or afraid you may never come back. My hope is that you will be with the elderly person for the rest of her life. Will you commit yourself to that?"

"I do," I said. I had not made this kind of a commitment to a person since I was married. Marilyn handed me an "Adoption Manual" to read.

"Keep the conversations light," she said. "Bring flowers for the adoptee to see and smell or articles from a magazine to discuss. Ask her questions about her past but try not to talk about how horrible her present conditions are. And the most important thing is to be dependable because your adoptee will be counting on you. Knowing you are coming back to visit will likely be the only thing the person has to look forward to all week. Just be positive. Like you are in your own life."

"When can I start?" I asked. Then I got nervous and reconsidered. What if I was committing myself for life to a person I couldn't stand being with for an hour?

"Don't worry," Marilyn said. "If it doesn't work out, you can just tell me after the first few visits. I need to connect you with someone very special. This should be a rewarding relationship for both of you. Just give me a few weeks. If I do my job right, I've got a feeling I'm going to make a perfect match for you."

THE PERFECT MATCH

Three weeks later I got a call from Marilyn. She had found someone for me. A woman. "She's very sharp. She takes good care of herself. She dresses very well. She's ninety-three, but she looks much younger. Her name is Adele. She's in excellent health except for one thing," Marilyn said. "She's blind."

I immediately got cold feet. This was partly because since I had met Marilyn, a woman in a new Mercedes drove into the back of my car while I was still in it and I had been in bed on ice ever since. Hearing that I had just adopted a blind person threw me. I had excitedly told almost everybody I knew that I was going to adopt an old lady, but the possibility of *this* happening never once crossed my mind. I felt ashamed, but I didn't appreciate Marilyn's idea of my perfect match. Blind woman, ninety-three, looks eighty-three sounded like the beginning of a badly written personal ad. Blind didn't sound like old. Blind sounded like burden.

"I think I should be able to walk by Saturday," I told Marilyn.

"Wonderful," she said. "Adele and I will see you at eleven. She lives at the California Chateau in the section that's a retirement hotel."

I didn't know exactly what a retirement hotel was, but I knew it had to be better than a "home" since hotel at least intimated the possibility of checking out.

Saturday morning I set out to meet Adele. The California Chateau was right across the driveway from a place called the Bel Air Manor Convalescent Home. The California Chateau was definitely the better-looking place to live. They had begonias and a big green awning that said "Welcome." The Manor had a sign that said "No parking. Paramedics only."

By the time I parked my car, I saw more old people outside within fifty feet than I had seen in all of L.A. in five years. This was a sanctuary for the elderly; across the street from the Rendezvous Hotel and kitty-corner from the Gun Shop.

I readjusted my neckbrace and walked slowly up the ramp to the Chateau. I knew I had to prepare myself for what I was going to see when I got inside, but I didn't know how to do that. I opened the door. There was a plastic marble desk and a ficus tree and a mural of what looked like the Northern California Wine Country. This wasn't bad at all. I saw Marilyn across the entryway, and she waved for me to follow her into a room with very bad wallpaper, a baby grand piano, and mint-green leather sofas. Adele was at the end of one of the sofas. A pretty, heavyset woman who introduced herself as Joanna, the Chateau administrator, got up off the sofa to let me sit beside Adele.

"You sure are popular today, Adele," Joanna said, winking at me.

"I am?" Adele asked. Her voice was too loud.

"Absolutely," Marilyn said. "Adele, this is Leah. Leah, Adele."

"Tell me who you are again?"

"Leah."

"Let her touch your neckbrace," Marilyn said. She took Adele's hand and placed it on my neck. "Leah was in a car accident," Marilyn said.

"Oh my," Adele said. "On her way over here?"

"No," I said. "In Beverly Hills. Last week."

I had never sat this close to a blind person before and I didn't know where I was supposed to look. Somehow she didn't seem blind. She did not have the skin of a ninety-three-year-old person. She was a nicely dressed old lady, very well put together as Marilyn had promised, with old-lady shoes, her pocketbook on her lap, a little wad of Kleenex, gray tufted hair, an average-size body, nondescript features, and a presence that was filling up the room. I didn't know if she could tell I was looking into her eyes, but I couldn't help it. I had never before seen a blind person wearing glasses—regular old lady glasses with prismed lenses that magnified her eyes. One moment they looked partially eclipsed with little blue lights. An instant later, they looked brown and then they were closed.

Adele's fingers moved back and forth on my neckbrace. Something in her touch told me she knew something deep about me—something I could never know.

"You're just wearing this to get attention," Adele finally said.

"That's right," I said. "Is it working?"

"What do you think?" Adele asked without missing a beat.

What I thought was that Marilyn was going to have to get me somebody else. This was my least favorite kind of old lady: brash, independent, with the sensitivity of a lout, who needed to be the center of attention, and who thought she could say whatever she wanted to say and get away with it because she was old.

Marilyn reached out for Adele's hand to show me how to make physical contact with the blind.

"Leah writes books for children," she said cheerfully.

"Really?" Adele asked with delight. "Books! That's marvelous! Oh, I love books! Do you know *Dick Wittington's Cat?*"

"I think I've heard of it," I said, lying. "What is it?"

"A book for children," Adele said. "I read it when I was little. I couldn't have been more than six. I can still see Dick Wittington's cat sitting on the steps of the church in the last picture." Adele smiled.

Just then a dog meandered into the room and stopped in front of the sofa. "Don't look now," I said. "But there's a dog in here."

"That's Vixen," the administrator said. "She lives here."

Vixen was a basset with skinny legs and the body of an expanding vacuum cleaner bag.

"Is that Vixen?" Adele cooed. She fumbled to open the clasp of her pocketbook. "Oh, I hope I have something for you in here, but I bet I don't."

"Here, Vixen," a woman wearing a Betty Boop T-shirt called from the next sofa.

Vixen lumbered over to the other sofa. "I have something for you, Vixen," Betty Boop said, breaking the plastic wrap off a jelly-roll.

"They treat dogs around here better than they do people," Adele said, taking me into her confidence.

"That's scary."

"Do you have children?" Adele asked abruptly.

"No, I don't."

"Well that's because you're young yet," Adele said. "You've got time."

I looked at Marilyn. I had just found something wonderful

14

about blindness, and I didn't know if I had to be honest and give it back.

"I can't get over how incredibly young you look, Adele," Marilyn said.

"You don't look ninety-three," I said.

"That's because I'm not ninety-three," Adele insisted. "I'm ninety-three and a half."

"That's remarkable." Marilyn beamed.

"It sure is," I said, even though I didn't know what ninety-three and a half was supposed to look like. All I knew was that we were a couple of adults encouraging an old lady to count her half birthdays like kids do who are under the age of ten.

"Is Saturday a good day for Leah to keep coming, Adele?" Marilyn asked. "I know you go to the Seniors' Center on Friday."

"Yes, that's right," Adele said. "Well, actually Tuesday, Wednesday, and Friday. And of course Monday is no good because Polly is here for our current events class."

"How about Thursday?" Marilyn asked.

"Well, no, Thursday Polly is here, too. And then of course Sunday someone comes from wherever they come to do my wash and help me take a bath. That sort of thing."

"How's Saturday?" I asked. "Saturday works for me."

"Yes, I suppose Saturday should be okay," Adele said. "Unless of course a visitor, maybe somebody from my family, comes to see me. But I suppose it's okay if you can be flexible."

"I'm flexible," I said trying to move my neck. I was getting impatient with this whole thing. I was here to give meaning to the life of some old person who had no one, and I was handed a blind woman with the social calendar of a debutante on speed.

"I'll come again next Saturday at eleven, Adele," I said, starting to get up.

"You know, it's interesting," Adele said, holding on to my hand. "My doctor here said I don't look ninety-three. Dr. Campbell. The first time I saw him he said, 'You don't look eighty!' Then he gave me a little kiss on my cheek."

"You could easily pass for eighty," Marilyn said.

"I suppose," Adele laughed. "But then when I saw the doctor the second time, he said, 'You don't look eighty, you could pass for seventy.' And he gave me another kiss on the cheek."

This was turning into an awakening: *nobody* believes they really look their age.

"You should go back and see him again," I said. "Maybe this time he'll tell you you look fifty."

"If Dr. Campbell tells me I look fifty, he's going to have to give me more than a kiss on the cheek!" Adele said.

Marilyn and I cracked up. Adele smiled and folded her hands over her pocketbook.

"You two really hit it off," Marilyn said, walking me to the door. She wished me good luck and said if she didn't hear from me, she'd call in about a month to see how things were going.

Right now things were going fine because I was outside. I was free. Eternity felt like it was easing up a little. I had done something good for somebody else, and if I didn't want to, I never had to do it again. Not that Adele was the worst first date I had ever had. In fact, she was one of the most intriguing. But I still couldn't think of being with her for the rest of her life. She looked like she might live too long for that. I just had to take this one Saturday at a time.

Joanna, the administrator, ran up to my car. Vixen followed behind her on the brink of cardiac arrest.

"I just want to thank you for volunteering," she said. "You have no idea what it means to one of our forgotten residents to have a visitor. Especially Adele."

"I'm happy to help," I smiled knowingly. "I hope I can make some small difference in Adele's life."

That was the least I could do given that she was about to totally change mine.

Leaving Your Home
at Ninety

The first Saturday that I was supposed to go see Adele alone, I overslept for one of the first times since I was a teenager and I left my house late, looking like a slob. This probably wouldn't have happened if I hadn't turned on KABC talk radio at midnight when my friend Zelie called to tell me astronomers were discussing a comet called Hale-Bopp that was coming our way with a spaceship attached, and I shouldn't miss it. Zelie was Jamaican. She had seen extraterrestrials and was totally relaxed with this news, but since I admittedly was a late bloomer to alien takeovers, by 3 A.M. I was a wreck. I kept telling Zelie if information like this got to the wrong ears, people would kill themselves.

Now I was driving to the California Chateau speeding down the side streets, which I never did, especially now that I was wearing a neckbrace and waiting to collide with a comet four times the size of the planet Earth. I was also nervous about walking back into that place. What would Adele and I have to talk about?

Inside the Chateau I was told that Adele was in the Chit Chat Room, the same room with the green leather sofas where we had met last week. I figured this was the place where everybody came to schmooze, although today nobody was talking it up except two women playing solitaire and a man on his walker backfiring a long round of gas. I saw Adele across the room. She seemed to be asleep on a sofa, sitting perfectly straight and smartly dressed, with her pocketbook tight in her hands. From a distance she looked sweeter and gentler today. I was thinking I should just leave when Adele woke up. I introduced myself again as it said to do in the Adoption Manual. I let Adele feel my neckbrace. Then I asked if I had come at a bad time.

Adele held her wristwatch to her ear and pushed a button. It was a talking watch with a man's voice. "It's 11:16 A.M.," the voice said.

"This isn't a bad time," Adele said too loudly. "However, this is the wrong time. Do I remember right that you said you'd be here at eleven o'clock?"

"Yes." It was just about eleven.

"Do you go by a watch?" Adele asked nicely.

Yeah, lady. Mine's got a little voice in it, too. If you turn up your hearing aid, you can hear it's screaming, "Get the hell out of here! You're not sixteen minutes late to a place like this. You're forty years too early. Besides, what difference does any of this make? Two more weeks and the whole planet could blow."

"I'm sorry," I heard myself say sincerely. "Next week I'll be here at exactly eleven o'clock," which was an insane promise since I never got anywhere exactly on time.

"That will be fine," Adele said. "Well, maybe you should call first. Next Saturday my family might be here at eleven." Adele's voice got much quieter. "I never know when they are coming."

I felt a sudden flurry of compassion for this woman who had nothing to hold on to but some hope.

"Will they be coming from far away?" I asked.

"That depends on what you call far away," Adele said. "Out of state or out of mind."

I asked Adele to tell me about her family. She told me she had three children. The youngest, Robert, lived in Reno. Her middle child, Edith, lived in Billings, Montana, and her oldest child, Violet, died here, Adele said, pointing to a spot on her shoulder.

"She was sitting right next to me on a sofa just like you are now and then the next thing I knew, she was gone. That was four years ago already."

"I'm so sorry," I said.

"Yup." Adele clenched the strap of her pocketbook. "It's utterly dead in here. Nobody in this place talks to me."

"Why not?"

"Because I'm blind!" Adele got impatient. " People think, 'She's blind so she must be dumb.'"

"That just sounds like ignorance to me," I said.

"Well of course it is," Adele said matter-of-factly. "I have my fair share of intelligence. I-N-T-E-L-L-I-G-E-N-C-E." I was impressed.

"Not bad for ninety-four." Adele smirked. "I'm not saying this just to boast, but I was always a spelling bee champion. Try telling anyone here that. Do you think that will make them give me the time of day?" Adele held her wrist to her ear. "It's eleven thirty and twenty seconds," the man said.

"Inconsequential," Adele said. "I-N-C-O-N-S-E-Q-U-E-N-T-I-A-L."

"Very good," I said.

"I can spell more," Adele offered.

I was beginning to remember how slowly time passed when it was just you alone with an old person. This was not the same old lady I met last week. The thrill was gone. What was I doing here? The millennium was hurtling to an end in what could be an intergalactic explosion of nitric gases, and I was sitting with someone who was phonetically spelling the word "rutabaga."

A woman in a Beatles cap passed us slowly and stared at me as if perhaps I didn't know Adele was blind. I had no idea this was how the blind were treated. I knew what it felt like to be ignored by others. I knew what it was like to be treated as if you had the cooties. But I knew this all as a child. I had seen it happen countless times when I visited kids in their grammar schools. I just had no idea this stuff still went on in the eightieth grade. Was I supposed to spend time here with Adele for the rest of her life only to learn that in the end nobody ever grows up?

I looked at Adele. How could anybody leave their parents in a place like this? I tried to imagine Adele's children, but it was a push to picture Adele as a mother; especially the kind of mother you'd feel comfortable enough to die on. I didn't know if I was going to make it through one whole hour with Adele, but I couldn't leave her, either. An old man went over to the piano and played "Sunrise, Sunset," and a woman with a nylon stocking on her head sat beside him on the bench and sang the words. Adele started to sing the words as if they were just part of our conversation. I looked around to see if anybody was looking, and then I sang, too. It was safe in here. This place was unthreatened by anything other than memories. "It's 11:40 and forty-two seconds," the man in the watch said. Adele felt for my hand. For a moment, I knew I was exactly where I was supposed to be.

At 11:59, however, I bounded out the door. I was vibrant and hot. I was aware and appreciative of how wonderful it was to be free in a way I could not remember having ever been before. I could move my fingers and toes quickly. I could drive far away. I felt guilty about leaving Adele behind, but I told myself she would understand in the way only old people could. I was a young girl. I had a life. I was going home and going back to bed.

*   *   *

The next Friday night I only stayed awake listening to Hale-Bopp radio until the experts said the comet would now miss colliding with Earth, although they suspected that the spaceship would still land here. The spaceship's purpose in stopping was not to harm us but to have its inhabitants teach us how to be more human, since it was obvious to them we didn't have a clue. This was less terrifying and made more sense to me, and I woke up the next morning feeling refreshed and hopeful that the planet would survive. I also hoped Adele wouldn't make a comment because I was showing up at her place at exactly 11:08.

"Did you forget something we talked about last week?" Adele asked, feeling her watch. "Tell me, do you remember *Dick Wittington's Cat?*"

"Wasn't that the book you told me you read as a child?"

"You remembered," Adele said with glee. "I've been thinking about that book since I met you. I can still visualize the last picture of the large church and the many white marble steps that went all the way up and across to the center of the church. Dick and his cat sat outside of the church on the left side, right there on the steps. Isn't it funny? Once you turn ninety, by golly, it's just as though you had it printed in front of you. You'll remember things from when you were five years old. But fifteen minutes back, you won't remember. That's normal."

Good, Adele, stay normal.

"I think I remembered DickWittington so clearly as a little girl because the steps of the church were very similar to the steps of the City Hall building in downtown Newark," Adele said. "That's New Jersey, see? I used to sit near the bottom of those steps, I don't know how many hours. I would just wait there patiently until my mother came to get me."

Adele told me that her mother was a suffragist for her friend Susan B. Anthony. Pearl, Adele's mother, rallied crowds to the top of the steps of the City Hall so they could listen to ongoing speeches and debates over the women's vote. Then when they were finished, Pearl went for her daughter who was waiting on a folding chair at the bottom of the steps and the two of them marched with the scores of other suffragettes.

Adele was too young to understand what was happening, but she knew it was something important. She could still remember holding on to the side of her mother's skirts as they paraded through the main streets of Newark, down Broad Street, across Market, and back up the white marble steps to the top of the City Hall. That was in 1909, eleven years before women got the vote and approximately eighty-four years before Adele first left New Jersey.

"My mother was quite a woman," Adele said. "She never gave up. My father, too, although he was a very different kind of person. He was hard-working but he was just a common laborer. My father and his sister and her little girl escaped from Russia. The little girl got lost in the woods. My father's sister prayed that a Russian farmer's wife would find her child and take her to live with them. Can you imagine how that small child must have felt?"

When I looked at Adele, I felt very bad, but right now all my imagination could conjure up was an asteroid traveling toward us, with a space caboose hanging off the end filled with extraterrestrial brain banks.

"And my father's father didn't even get out of Russia," Adele said. "They had ways of existence we couldn't begin to dream of as we sit here living our secure lives. They had the guts. Of course, I wouldn't wish this kind of living here on anyone."

"This is not your idea of a good time, right?"

"This wasn't my idea at all," Adele said. "In my wildest dreams I never thought I'd end up in a place like this."

And then in 1993, when Adele was ninety, she told me she drove across country with Edith, Violet, and Violet's dog. They were moving west to Southern California. Robert had already moved to Riverside County. When Violet and Edith decided they had had enough of the East Coast winters too, there was no way they were going to let Adele stay behind. Violet found a little house for her and Adele not far from Robert's and Edith's houses. Then everything was shipped out from New Jersey. One hot December afternoon, Violet took a break from unpacking boxes and she sat on the sofa next to her mother. She rested her head on Adele's shoulder to take a little nap. Seconds later Violet had a stroke and massive heart attack and died on her mother's arm.

"It was so fast," Adele said. "Everything moved so fast."

"That must have been a terrible shock," I said.

"Oh yes, it was," Adele said bravely. "Your whole life can change on a dime."

A few months after Violet's death, Robert discovered opportunities were better for him in Reno and Edith got a job in Billings where her overhead could be much cheaper. Before they moved, they drove Adele down to L.A. to the California Chateau where she has lived ever since.

"Yup." Adele sighed. "And I hadn't gone completely blind yet. I still had a very little vision left when I came here. Only God in heaven knows why He wanted me to come to California."

"I know what you mean," I said. Then we just sat there in silence. I thought of Violet. I had to get up off that sofa. I had to figure out what to say to make my way out of there.

"Isn't it time for you to go?" Adele caught me off guard. She lifted her watch to her ear. "It's 11:52 and forty seconds," the man said.

"Should I just meet you right here again next week?" Adele asked.

"Sure," I said "I'll be back next Saturday at eleven. Is the same time all right?"

"I suppose the same time is all right," Adele said, feeling my hand. "But it would be better if it were the right time. Which is not 11:08. Am I right?"

Of course she was right. "Was I late?" I laughed. "I can't believe this. You busted me."

"Sure I did." Adele smirked. "Doesn't that just get your goat?"

*   *   *

That night I was at a dinner party at my friend Brenda's with some of her affected friends from the film business, and I started thinking about Adele. I couldn't stop picturing her in that moment alone on the sofa, dressed like a lady, with her eyes fluttering behind her glasses like two lost birds. In a few hours I could leave here and go home, but Adele was never going to find her way home again. I realized Adele was the oldest person I had ever met, and she was perhaps from the most innocent generation alive. She was the last of the generation of Americans who left their homes and went out in the world on their own for the first time at ninety. Adele expected and wanted to live her entire life with her family, and she almost made it through. She went from the house she was born in to the house where she was married to the house where she raised her family to the houses her children lived in when Adele was widowed. Finally she went to the California Chateau, where she had to learn how to live alone, just in time to die.

Adele was not your regular L.A. girl. She didn't come here for pilot season. She came here to be with her family. But if you wanted to talk about your feature film with the twenty million dollars' worth of special effects, Adele was twenty-seven when the first "talkie" came out. She heard the very first radio broadcast show. Her family was the second on their block to get a telephone. She was around for vaudeville and two world wars and the Great Depression—the one before Prozac. What was she doing living in a home? She should be living in the Smithsonian.

"And yet fundamentally I guess her kids did the best they could by putting her where they did," I said to the young producer sitting next to me at the dinner table.

"Probably," the man said, helping himself to my wineglass. "But I'd rather be abducted by aliens than walk into a place like that."

*   *   *

The next Saturday I left for Adele's, a little blown out from the week like the rest of the country. Hale-Bopp first became visible in the sky, and thirty-nine people from a cult called Heaven's Gate took that as their sign that it was time to pack the bags, put on their Nikes, swallow some phenobarbital, and leave home for the next dimension.

So what was I supposed to talk to Adele about today? I pulled into the Chateau driveway thinking about those thirty-nine people living and dying in a villa in Rancho Santa Fe and the one woman whose suicide note said, "I've lived on this planet thirty-one years and there's nothing here for me." How would I explain that to a woman who was blind, six years shy of a century, and still out of bed every morning putting on panty hose? I decided the best thing to say was nothing.

"So did you hear about those spaceship people who committed suicide?" Adele asked as soon as I sat down beside her.

"Yes," I said. "What a tragedy."

It was horrible, all right. Some of those people hadn't been allowed to see their families for almost twenty years. "Yup"—Adele shook her head—"such is life."

You Make Me Feel So Younger

By Monday of the following week I was beginning to have a sinking, all-over feeling that I had "done" Adele. It's not that she wasn't an interesting woman, but I had gotten the whole picture. Adopting Adele was not going to be bigger than life. It was just adopting Adele. All adoption meant was that once a week I would get to sit beside a really old lady on a sofa and sink faster into my future than anyone else my age. Seeing Adele was not going to save me from fearing the Golden Years later. There were no Golden Years coming down the pike. There was nothing golden about them. *These* were them, and there had to be a better place to spend them than at the California Chateau. I was a fast study. I had gotten every lesson there was for me to get out of this relationship.

I felt ashamed that my commitment to be dependable couldn't be counted on, but the only responsible thing to do now was call Marilyn at the Elder Corps. If I could get out of my marriage, I could get out of anything. Besides, Adele would be okay. She wasn't going to kick the bucket after ninety-three years because I stopped visiting her after three weeks.

I was looking up Marilyn's number when Jenny called me from her car phone.

"How's the old lady?" she asked. "I was thinking it's so nice that you're still seeing her. She must love you. I wish I had the time to do something like that, but I don't have time now to go to the bathroom. You always had the kindest heart. Ever since the third grade."

I swallowed hard. Then I tried to explain to Jenny that Adele was terrific but I was getting ready to bail.

"Don't do it," Jenny said. "This is something special. I know it may not be so easy being around a bunch of old people, but who knows? Maybe you're going to meet somebody's grandson in that place. Maybe there's a wonderful doctor to marry right under your nose; not that marriage is the biggest miracle that could come out of a relationship. But I have a good feeling. Please trust me on this one. Don't quit yet. Just give it one more try."

I took Jenny's call to be the sign that I was, in fact, to give it another try. The key word here was try. How hard had I really been trying to make this relationship work? I felt renewed and jazzed to go back and read the Adoption Manual—really read it for the first time. It said, "Occasionally bring adoptees an item such as a flower to smell or some special material to touch that will help keep them engaged in life." I smiled. Whoever wrote this thing didn't know Adele. It was going to take a lot more than a flower to keep her engaged in life. There was only one perfect thing I could think of that would do the trick. I had to bring Adele *Dick Wittington's Cat*.

The chances of finding an obscure out-of-print children's book from the early 1900s are on a par with stumbling over the remains of Jimmy Hoffa. It was not likely to happen, but somehow I had the belief it could be done. Not only was I going to bring Adele that book, but I pledged to myself that she would have it Saturday morning by eleven o'clock.

I found myself having energy the likes of which I hadn't experienced since the days when I lived in New York and got a weekly B-12 shot. The more I looked for the book, the more I imagined the joy it would bring to Adele when she held it in her hands.

By Thursday I had called in every book contact and favor I could think of, but *Dick Wittington* was nowhere to be found. It crossed my mind that Adele couldn't see to know if I was bringing her *Dick Wittington's Cat* or *The Cat in the Hat Came Back.* So what difference did it make really? It was the difference between faith and the real world.

The real world didn't care about *Dick Wittington's Cat.* It didn't care that a person could live ninety-three years and in the end be moved most dearly by remembering a single book from her childhood. It didn't care that a printed page and a picture were not forgotten from the time a mother first read it aloud, or that it could reconnect a person with a lifetime of personal history. It didn't care that therefore out of basic human respect a book should not be allowed to be taken away forever from a person's reach. The real world didn't know what it meant to revere the simple and the remarkable. Things had to move too fast now for anyone to care about that. I felt saddened and ashamed that this was true, but there was nothing more I could do about it.

Then Friday afternoon I got a call from an antiquarian bookseller/ammunitions agent in San Bernardino. He said he had what he was sure was the only copy of *Dick Wittington and His Cat* in existence. I could have it mailed to me by Tuesday, or I could come pick it up before five. San Bernardino is a cowboy town two hours outside of L.A., and on the up chance you hit no traffic you could get there in two hours. Otherwise you were looking at anywhere from three hours to a week. I had never been there before, and at no other time in my L.A. life had I ever undertaken a Friday afternoon driving trek much farther than the dry cleaners. But today was a day of victory. Tomorrow morning I was going to make Adele very happy.

I got to the bookstore/ammo shop at 4:45. The dealer turned out to be about twenty and adorable, and when he put *Dick Wittington and His Cat* on the counter, he smiled right at me. There was a picture of a church and it had the steps just as Adele had described it, but the book didn't look that old to me. I figured it just had to be a reprint.

"Sure it is," the bookseller pointed out. "You're going to be hard put to find many books outside the Bible today that are older than that. Christ! Look at that copyright. Do you know how old that book is already?"

Of course I did. It was my age.

"Get out of town!" The boy laughed. "No, it's not. I mean, what are you? Thirty?"

Yes, I was. For the first time in years I had my whole life ahead of me. I was driving down the freeway going seventy with the oldies station blasting at full volume. *Dick Wittington and His Cat* were bopping up and down in the backseat. I was happier about being around a kid's book than I had been for years. The song "Searching for My Love" by Bobby Moore was on the radio. Memories from the seventies and then the sixties were flooding back to me. I was singing, "I'm searching, searching, searching for my baby." Yes, I was. Life was good.

Saturday morning I walked into the Chit Chat Room at ten after eleven, beaming. The room was packed. An old guy wearing a base-ball cap was at the piano playing bad honky-tonk and the joint could have been jumping if three-quarters of the people in it weren't half dead.

I couldn't see Adele, and then I finally spotted her sitting at the end of a sofa with two other people on it. A man on the sofa saw me and motioned for me with his cane to come over. I didn't want to take a seat from an old person, but now the man was showing me how, if he scootched down, there would be enough room for me to squeeze in between him and Adele. For a moment I felt like a little girl again: trapped into bringing a little sunshine into the world of old people and just hoping that before I could get out of there they wouldn't start to smell. I told Adele I had a surprise for her, and then I slowly put the book into her hands.

"What is it?" she asked. "A book?"

"It's *the* book," I tried to say without squealing with delight. "I give you *Dick Wittington and His Cat.*"

"Really?" Adele said too loudly. "Well, I'll be!" Her whole face filled with so much light that it was almost embarrassing to see an old person so elated. She felt around the edges of the book binding. Then she put the book under her nose. The other people on the sofa just stared.

"Mine was new," Adele said dreamily. "It had a delicious smell that only a new book can have. And it had gold-embossed lettering that stood up off the book." Adele tried to feel the letters in the title. "Will you read it to me? And go slowly!"

I opened the book and started reading. Although the story was maudlin, the moment between Adele and me was tender until Adele stopped me abruptly to tell me she didn't remember this. Not a word of what I was reading was coming back to her.

"What did you say the name of this book is again?" Adele asked.

"Dick Wittington and His Cat." I pronounced each word carefully.

"Oh then, no wonder," Adele said very matter-of-factly. "That explains everything! This is *Dick Wittington and His Cat.* The name of my book was *Dick Wittington's Cat.*"

I tried to explain to Adele that this had to be the same book and that it was just a reprint because things in the world change over time and she probably just didn't remember.

"No," she said. "This just isn't the book, that's all."

There was no arguing with her. She remembered the exact book. I couldn't remember the exact title. I was humbled and I was ready to get out of there.

"What about the Library of Congress?" Adele asked. "They know the name of every book that was ever published. And they have a copy of it, too. Have you thought of them?"

The truth was the Library of Congress hadn't even crossed my mind.

"Have you considered calling them on the telephone? They're in Washington, D.C."

The only place I was considering calling was the Elder Corps so I could talk to Marilyn. I had given it one more try. This old lady didn't need me. If I was going to do this, I needed a sweet little old granny who could see enough so that when I came into her view a twinkle came into her eyes and her heart overflowed with gratitude. Now Adele and I just sat there on the sofa. We sat there for what seemed like a very long time.

Then finally something happened that would change my relationship with Adele forever—we got up off the sofa. Adele invited me to walk her to lunch. She put out her arm for me to hold and then she opened a cane from her pocketbook and tapped it out in front of her. It was past my time to leave, but I was about to take my first peek at the Chateau outside of the Chit Chat Room.

*   *   *

"When we get to the tree, that's when I know to go left," Adele said. "Come on. I'll give you the tour, but we'd better step on it. We eat at twelve-thirty. They line up."

It was ten after twelve when we started down a long empty corridor with lots of closed doors and wallpaper that looked like pink TV static. Adele was sturdy and I felt amazingly at ease with her until we got to the end of the hallway, passed the Pepsi machine, and walked smack dab into the lineup. There was no backing up and no way out ahead because the line was an expanding glob of glazed-over-looking old people that dead-ended into the dining room, and the dining room doors were locked.

"Are we there yet?" Adele asked too loudly.

A woman in her early seventies with the poise of a warthog yanked on the dining room doors. "I don't know what their problem is in there today," she grunted. "It's not that they don't know what time we eat. This is ridiculous."

"That woman has a big, fat mouth," Adele tried to whisper. "She thinks that makes her leader of the house. God forbid that this is any kind of house."

This was some kind of a house all right. Wherever two or more were gathered three times a day to eat a meal there was going to be a home. It struck me in that moment that it might have killed Adele if she could see that this was her final family: old, lost, and unwanted souls stranded together outside the dining room door. Just then the doors opened.

"Walkers and canes first," the warthog called, coming right at us. "I'll take her," she said, putting her hand out to Adele. "Don't worry, I always take her in." The warthog mouthed out each word with exaggeration so Adele couldn't see. "It's awful that she's blind. I feel so sorry for her."

"Sarah?" Adele asked, reaching for the warthog's arm. Suddenly I didn't want to let Adele go.

"I hate to give you the bum's rush, Leah," Adele joked. "But get out of here. And I thank you very much for making the effort to bring me that book. Do you think you would have the time to find the real book for next time?"

"I may be able to find the time," I said. "But I'm afraid it's going to take a miracle to find that book."

"But if you have the time, you should expect a miracle," Adele said with the fervor of a football coach. "Of course you should. And that's the truth! You're much too young not to expect a miracle."

"I suppose you're right." I laughed.

"Bye-bye for now," Adele said, walking into the dining room. "I'll see you next week."

The miracle was that I was certain now there was going to be a next week. If I was lucky, Adele would forget about *Dick Wittington* by then. I didn't know who this woman was, but I knew she was in my life on Saturdays. What I didn't know then was soon I would be at the Chateau on Mondays, Wednesdays, and Fridays as well. I was about to become a "regular."

PART TWO

A Home for the Aging

ADELE'S ROOM

It was on my sixth visit when Adele first asked if I wanted to leave the Chit Chat Room and go back to her place. I thought of my grandmother's room at the Darrow Plaza Home where she died. Suddenly the Chit Chat Room looked very good to me. Adele opened her cane and tapped it out in front of her.

"I have one of the best locations," Adele said proudly. "Come on. I'll show you the way."

Adele's room was the first one down the hallway past the mailboxes, after the special events bulletin board and directly across from the drugs closet. I tried to prepare myself for what I would see when Adele finally got her key into the lock.

I saw my grandmother's room with the table on wheels where she kept all she had left of her belongings: a silver spit pan, her jar of colored sucking candies, and a photograph of all of the grandchildren taken when we were in junior high. It was as if she had no memory that she once had owned a houseful of beautiful things and antiques that nobody was ever invited in to see. And now, all she had was an orange Naugahyde chair that came with the room and the hope that somebody from outside would come and sit in it.

"It's a modest room," Adele said, turning the knob. "But you're welcome."

The inside of Adele's room was wall-to-wall furniture that came in twos like an ark built for old people. There were two twin beds with two matching faded quilts, two mirrored dressers beside two pink Naugahyde chairs, and two nightstands with two orange lamps on them that looked like they cost two dollars each.

One thing was undeniable: Adele may have been living in a hotel with rented early Howard Johnson's furniture, but I actually owned pieces that looked remarkably like this. I was only planning on having it temporarily. Now more than half my life was over, and I was still living as if it was just a matter of time before the delivery truck showed up with my real stuff. Privately I lived with a chronic terror that I would never be able to remodel what I had without the help of a sizable drug heist. I had subconsciously fallen into the habit of socializing at the homes of my friends who had *real* houses. Less and less did I want anybody in mine. I knew it was superficial and spiritually dwarfed, but I had been sinking deeper and deeper into this pattern. Adele's room was forcing me to face this pathetic truth. I wanted to run.

"Make yourself at home," Adele said, feeling her way over to the pink Naugahyde chair. There was a yellow wooden rocker crammed in beside it that obviously didn't come with the room. Adele ran her hands on the slats of the seat. "Be my guest," she said. "Park your carcass. This is my sitting chair. Go ahead. Sit in it! I'll sit in the other. It's a very good chair. My daughters bought it for me."

"It's a really nice chair," I said. "This is a nice room."

"Yes, it's pleasant enough." Adele smiled up at the ceiling. "With the way it's decorated and all."

I looked around. The walls were completely bare. There wasn't a plant or knickknack or a spit pan or a telephone. There was a sliding glass door that looked out onto the driveway and was covered by a bad generic drape. It dawned on me that perhaps what I was witnessing was the true way to spiritual freedom—blindness.

"I haven't always been this blind," Adele said. "I could still see certain things until I moved in here. Then God had me go total."

God was a merciful peach.

"Does it seem dark in here to you?" Adele asked. "I keep the curtains closed so nobody looks in from the outside."

How could she see who, if anybody, was looking in on her? It hit me that I had no idea what it was Adele saw, if anything, other than total blackness. I had just always felt like she was somehow, in some way, seeing me.

"Wallpaper," Adele said. "All I see is wallpaper." She pointed out the pattern in front of her. "Sometime I will tell you how I started losing my sight many years ago. Yup." Adele sighed. "I was just a youngster. Can I offer you a chocolate macaroon?"

There was something familiarly desperate about being offered a treat in the room of an old person. I flashed on the many times my grandmother held out her glass jar and told me to take one of her sucking candies. It was as if she had no recollection that she used to bribe me with cakes and bicycles and knit me suits and buy me shares of AT&T. She wanted me to have the piece of candy. One cherry ball wrapped in cellophane was at the heart of everything she had ever wanted to give. I had to take it.

Adele did not seem like that kind of old lady. She did not even look like she belonged in this room. She looked larger and more regal than all this. Still I wasn't sure. I didn't know if I had to eat the macaroon to validate her existence.

"If you don't want it, would you mind putting this away for me?"

Adele asked, taking the macaroon from her pocketbook. "You'll have to hide it so nobody comes and steals it."

Who would steal a macaroon? What happens to an old person's mind that allows her the ability to turn back into a little child who has found one special pebble that she is devoted to loving and protecting as if it is the most sought-after treasure on earth?

"It goes in the top right drawer in my dresser," Adele instructed me. "Mine's the one when you walk straight. The other dresser belongs to my roommate if I ever get one. Go ahead. I trust you."

I wanted to simply hide the macaroon and close the drawer, but I couldn't. There was no place in the drawer to hide it. All that was in this dresser now was a tin full of salt packets, a printing stamp that appeared to be in Braille, a man's black plastic comb, and a small box of safety pins. In the end, my grandmother had nothing, too, but she had gone to the Darrow Plaza to die. Adele was here to live until she died. She was fifteen years older than my grandmother and healthy. She should have had more valuables.

When I walked back to Adele, I noticed for the first time a safety pin in the hem of her pants. It looked as if it had been stuck there by mistake. I figured somebody had forgotten to remove the pin when they brought the pants back to Adele from the cleaners. Adele pushed up her sweater sleeve, and there was a safety pin on the inside of the material there, too.

"If the pin is going sideways, that means these are dark-colored winter pants," Adele said. "A single up and down pin is a sweater, also dark but always matching. It always has to be an outfit. Like this one. It matches, right?"

"Perfectly," I said.

"These are my black pants and this is my gray top, right?"

"Exactly," I said.

"Of course," Adele smiled. "The pins are how I know which clothes to pick out in the morning."

It had not occurred to me that someone didn't just come in every morning and pick out Adele's clothes for her. She was proud and completely on her own.

"I don't mind telling you I don't relish the aloneness," Adele said. "One day you wake up and you're utterly by yourself. You don't want to spend your whole life like that. It's good to live with someone if only to be able to ask, 'Does this blouse match?' Or, 'What color is this vest?' My old roommate, Sally, did that for me. She was a very nice person. She died."

"I'm sorry," I said.

I could not begin to imagine how much courage it took for Adele just to make it through a day. How much self-respect did a person have to have to be ninety-three and a half, blind, and meticulous about her wardrobe when she couldn't even see inside her closet? For what reason could this woman convince herself it was worth it to wake up and look good every day?

"I think you're remarkable," I said. "Did it take a long time for someone to teach you the system with the pins?"

"Nobody taught me that." Adele laughed. "No. I made the pin thing up when I came to live here. I had to. It's amazing the things you find yourself doing in your life that you never dreamed you would do until you have to do them. Yup." Adele ran her fingers over a pin. She smiled a smile of deep satisfaction. "You can learn in the smallest things."

Across the room in the dresser mirror I saw Adele and myself sitting. Adele felt for my hand. I rocked. I looked like I belonged in that chair. I was going to be learning a lot in that room.

ARMCHAIR TRAVELING

The next Saturday morning, Jenny called on her car phone. She was on her way to her second meeting of the day, and I was getting ready to leave for Adele's.

"Promise me when we get old we won't be in a place like that," I said. "All the people do where she lives is eat, sleep, and watch TV."

"Oh my God," Jenny said. "Doesn't that just sound like the best vacation?"

When I walked into the Chateau, I could hear the theme song from the movie *Love Story* blaring out from the Chit Chat Room. The movie was on TV, and the TV area was packed to the gills. I went in there looking for Adele, but nobody seemed to even notice me. Ray Milland was warning his preppy son Ryan O'Neal that if he married Ali MacGraw, Milland wouldn't give him the time of day; and a fight was about to break out on one of the sofas. A man wanted to change the channel, and a woman who looked like a bulldozer in a muumuu wasn't going to stand for that.

"You always pick the channel," the man tried to scold her. "You don't go anywhere. All you do is sit on your ass all day."

"I do not," the bulldozer shouted. "I have a job! I used to sell real estate!"

I had to get out of there. I finally spotted Adele completely alone on a sofa across the room. She looked like she had just been left or forgotten. For a second I wanted to cry. Adele was too good for those people. How could people live so long and still be so cruel? I had been with Adele alone in her room, and I never wanted to have to see her alone among people again. How was I supposed to honor the feelings she must have been having at that moment and buffer her from those same feelings at the same time? They didn't print that in the Adoption Manual.

Adele was nicely dressed with her pocketbook held tightly across her lap. She was looking upward as if she was watching a private screening of the movie on the ceiling.

"Are you listening to the movie?" I asked when I sat down beside her.

"Movie? No. I was just listening to whales," Adele smiled. "They are quite remarkable animals. Did you know that whales can converse with each other under water from a hundred miles away?"

"I had no idea."

"Yup." Adele held my hand. Her fingers were warm and strong. "I was just remembering how I traveled the ocean with whales. It was in the Atlantic. A whale was giving birth. The whales all stick together. See? They circle around the mother to protect her. And that's how it used to be with people, you know. Of course families were families in those days." Adele's voice got quiet. "Today the children go separate."

I remembered my job was to keep the conversation positive. "When were you in the Atlantic?"

"Oh, it wasn't that terribly long ago," Adele said. "Of course time goes by. You should make sure you travel and see all you want to see and more while you still have the physical ways and means to do it."

"That's good advice," I said.

"Well, it's true," Adele said. "Of course you're still young."

"I'm not that young. Have you done much traveling?"

"Oh, yes. I'm what you call a bookworm. I've traveled all around the world in my armchair. I walked from Asia to America before it was called America and then up into Alaska. I walked and I walked when I could hardly walk anymore. This man I read about used his own feet—all the way up to the Arctic Circle. Oh, I enjoyed that kind of travel—Asia, Asia Minor."

"When was the last time you read?"

"What do you mean? I was reading in my rocker before I came down here. Do you know the author Guy de Maupassant? Have you ever read *Devil's Island*?"

"No, I haven't," I said. "I read one of his short stories in college. I don't remember the name." The truth was I couldn't remember the last work of fiction I read cover to cover.

"Oh, you shouldn't wait. Remember the name. *Devil's Island*. It's a wonderful book. I also love Louis L'Amour. You've read his books, haven't you?"

"I don't think so," I said. "Do you read in Braille?"

"No. I learned but I didn't like it. I listen to the talking books instead. They send them to me from the Braille Institute and they give me a talking machine, and then when I'm done with the books I send them back. I like hearing the voice. I have liked books that take you exploring. I traveled north. I went to Hawaii before it was Hawaii and it was a gigantic rock. I traveled to a spot in Israel. I was there when

God gave Moses the Ten Commandments. They planted flowers all around the Commandments. I was there because I could visualize it!"

I was enchanted. "May I come to your room and see some of your books on tape? I'm curious."

"I suppose I have a few minutes before lunch," Adele said. "Let's get out of here."

Adele reached for her cane, took it out of her purse, and started to open it.

"Do I need this?"

"No, not if you'll let me guide you," I said.

"If you wish."

Adele took my arm. We passed the TV area. Some people looked up.

"This place has absolutely, extremely little entertainment," Adele said. "I hope I've used enough adjectives."

"You've painted a picture." I laughed. This woman deserved all the positive support in the world.

"I was always a people person. And now here I am at this place utterly alone. Thank God I have my books to console me."

I knew what she meant. "Sometimes I feel that way about the books I have written."

"Yes, but you have a very special talent," Adele said. "You have to be born to write. You have to build up a big vocabulary."

"Yeah, and that's just the swear words." I laughed.

"That must make you feel so proud," Adele said.

"Quite frankly, I'm feeling a little burned out," I said reluctantly.

"What is that?" Adele asked. She had obviously never heard the expression. I felt like a spoiled brat telling this to a woman who probably never had been burned out a day in her life until she came to this place. But I couldn't stop now.

"Burned out means you've done it," I said. "The thrill is gone. You're tired of it."

"Oh." Adele thought for a second. "Could it possibly mean that it is just time to try writing something different? Do you know how I would feel if I held a book in my hands that I wrote?"

"How?"

"Exultant."

*   *   *

By the time we reached Adele's room I felt young, and the idea of writing was thrilling me. There was a cassette player on the counter, and Adele felt her way over to the rocking chair and handed me a green plastic box with a tape in it.

"What's this?" Adele asked.

"It says it's called 'Intimate Grammar.'"

"They sent me this from Braille. Like I need this in here."

"Well, you never know," I said. "Some cute guy might be right under your nose here. With this book you'll be prepared."

"If you say so," Adele said. "Believe me, they should have some-one in their nineties write a book like this. They've had the experi-ence. I know a thing or two. You can bet your life I do."

"Oh, I believe it. I bet you could write a great book."

"Of course," Adele said matter-of-factly.

"What would your title be?"

"Enjoy Yourself While You Can," Adele said without missing a beat.

"And how long is that?"

"Until you die."

FOOD IS IT!

By Wednesday of the following week I was already waiting for Saturday. Then Saturday morning, Adele and I were in the Chit Chat Room again. She was telling me about a book she was listening to on tape about ants. I could not believe how quickly the hour seemed to be passing. Adele's face filled with light.

"I was reading how, out of the millions and millions of ants, each group has its own job, like building a colony or transporting its young. And don't you think it's astounding that even the tiniest pinpoint of a little bit of life like an ant can follow through with all of that purpose before it dies?"

Yes, I did. I found it absolutely amazing my purpose was to add a little bit of meaning to Adele's day and she was expanding my whole vision of life. I had never heard an old person speak with such almost-embarrassing enthusiasm. Adele was a poet, and I was a little girl again just hanging on to her every word.

Adele lifted her talking watch to her ear. "Oh my God in heaven," she gasped. "It's twelve-fifteen already. We eat in fifteen minutes."

The spell was broken and I didn't like it. Now I had to care for her. I had to be the voice of clear adult thinking.

"It's okay," I said slowly and deliberately. "You still have plenty of time. Besides, have you ever missed a meal?"

"No," Adele said. "And I don't want there to be a first time."

Adele lifted herself from the sofa. She let me take her arm. Then we headed for the dining room. A woman on a walker with tennis balls on its feet passed us on the left.

"Is the food here pretty good?" I asked Adele, trying to maintain any conversation. Adele didn't answer. She was saving her breath for picking up the pace. It made me sad that within a matter of seconds I had seen Adele transform from extraordinary to any other old person in that place. Her only purpose now was to keep the faith that the lineup was straight ahead and another meal around the corner.

Looking out over that hallway and the horizon of my life, it hit me that in the end I would know life's purpose never changes. The difference between what I had now in my middle-aged meals and what Adele would never have again was the freedom to pick my own restaurant. I could still choose. I did not have to eat in the same place twice if I didn't want to or with the same person more than once if I couldn't stomach it. I had taken for granted that I would forever hold these options as my inalienable rights. Suddenly the thought of losing control of my food was more terrifying than losing control of my bowels.

"I wonder what we're having to eat," Adele asked me, like I knew the menu.

A man wearing a Nike cap backward walked up to a bulletin board, put his face almost completely up against it, and began reading. "Hawaiian Chicken. Hey, folks," he called. "Make like an elephant and pack your trunk. We're headed for Hawaii. A-lo-ha-hoi, A-lo-ha-hoi," he hula-ed through the crowd. Adele and I were the only ones who laughed. There was hope here. This man had the right idea. Maybe there was some entertainment with these meals.

"Shut up, Johnny," the warthog snapped at the hula man. The warthog was guarding the dining room doors. "Nobody appreciates your ruining their appetite before we go in for dinner."

"Ah, the hell with all of you." The man turned mean. "Seven years I've lived in this place. Somebody get me a .45."

Nobody said a word. "That's Johnny." Adele tried to whisper. "Everybody thinks he's sort of a troublemaker. He sits at my table."

I didn't want to try to pick out the rest of the people they had put at Adele's table or envision what they would look like eating. I didn't want to be so fearful as to believe there could come a day when anybody would actually give a .45 to Johnny except that gun shop across the street. I couldn't allow myself to wrap my mind around an image as horrendous as the day when I would actually know what Hawaiian Chicken was and I would run to eat it anyway. All I was going to do was drop Adele off and get out of there.

The warthog opened the dining room doors so the lineup could start to move. Suddenly an elevator door opened behind me and wheelchairs came pouring out. I was standing there and it was muggy and hot, with nothing but old people staring ahead, and it occurred to me that for the first time in my life I might faint. I kept looking for the warthog to come and take Adele, but when she finally caught my eye it was only to mouth out the words: "You can take Adele in today. We let her in first with the cripples."

"Are we going in yet?" Adele asked. "My table is the first one when you get inside."

Good. That was as far in as I could go. I didn't belong. It had to be something like a private club in there. I could not watch a grown woman having a bib tied around her neck. I didn't want to see people at the end of their lives sit right across from each other and say absolutely nothing. I didn't want to see that someday I could be one of these people and I wouldn't remember that was supposed to bother me. I didn't want to know that if push came to shove I could chew with my seven remaining teeth. I didn't want to live to see the day I would not be deemed safe to prepare my own meals. I didn't want to eat foods that I didn't get to feel raw first at the grocery store. I didn't want to have to see the day when I would be forced to watch a lifetime of healthy eating go down the toilet because all the foods I had rigorously avoided in order to live a long life were the very foods I had to eat now before they would let me die.

Adele and I found her chair. Two women in hair nets came around pushing food carts, and I couldn't get through them to slip back out the doorway. They poured Adele a cup of coffee from a pot that smelled like it had been sitting since the beginning of time. Then they served the coleslaw and desserts first, giving the idea that those dishes were most of what everyone was going to eat anyway. Today the dessert was chocolate crème pie. I couldn't see any crust on Adele's plate. It was all aerosol crème piled high. How was Adele supposed to eat that with any shred of dignity without being able to see it? I looked at Adele's piece. I hadn't stood that close to a piece of chocolate crème pie in years. It didn't look so bad. What if, in the end, it looked good and all I wanted to eat was chocolate crème pie? Who would I have in my life to stop me? What if none of my last wishes were honored and they buried me ten feet under with white sugar and red meat in my bloodstream? How the hell would I rest in peace knowing I saw this all coming thirty years earlier and couldn't do anything to stop it? How could Adele make it through one day of this existence?

I looked over and saw Adele counting the spaces on the table with her fingers to feel for her utensils. Then she silently and methodically turned them all around so that the big spoon was first, then the fork, then the little spoon and the knife. She was gaining some control.

"There." She smiled. "I rearrange all of this to my liking."

"You're smart," I told her.

"Ain't I though." She laughed. "If you can be dumb or you can be smart, you might as well be smart."

"Smart is smart," I said.

"You're my kind of gal." Adele squeezed my hand.

I could leave now. I knew Adele was where she was supposed to be. But I didn't want to leave her there.

"Bye-bye," Adele said.

"Okay," I said. "I'll leave you. I'm sure you must be hungry."

"Hungry?" Adele swallowed her first spoonful of pie. "Oh, no. I'm never hungry in this place when they serve. But what am I going to do? You've got to eat!"

A Gentleman Caller

Friday I was dressing for a first date with an attorney I had been fixed up with by my friend Cheryl, and I couldn't get my mind off Adele. I felt guilty that I had an evening of possibility ahead of me but the only possibility for Adele was the dining room. I kept seeing what she looked like when I left her sitting alone at her table.

I comforted myself by remembering I was not Adele's granddaughter and by believing Adele knew something that I was still too young to grasp. Old people have an innate ability to accept even the most monotonous of their circumstances. They derive their pleasure from watching young people enjoy their lives. Knowing I had a good time tonight would bring Adele great happiness tomorrow.

The lawyer picked me up in his Beamer that he kept telling me he paid for in cash, and he joked that if I looked inside the glove compartment I'd find a deck of playing cards we could take with us into the restaurant in case things got dull during dinner. Halfway through the meal it was time to crack open the deck.

The next morning I was excited to go to Adele's. I decided to surprise her by getting there early so she could have a little extra time not being alone. When I got to the Chateau, Adele was not in the Chit

Chat Room so I headed down the hallway. From inside Adele's room I could hear a man's voice singing, which I figured was part of a talking book Adele was listening to. I knocked louder so she could hear me. When Adele finally came to the door, her glasses were off and she was laughing. I could see a man leaning against the dresser in her room.

"Frank, this is Leah," Adele said, feeling for my hand. "Leah, Frank."

Frank had jet-black hair like Elvis's and the nose and glasses of Mr. Potato Head. He was wearing a very Hawaiian shirt, red short-shorts, black ankle socks, and wing-tipped shoes. He smiled and looked me square in the eye. The most bizarre thing about him was that he probably wasn't much older than I was. Apparently, you didn't necessarily have to be old to live in a retirement hotel—you could be just cracked enough that your family wanted you gone at fifty.

"I was just here rehearsing for Adele," Frank said, like he was explaining himself to Adele's mother.

"Frank has a beautiful voice," Adele told me. "He used to take lessons with Barbra Streisand's old teacher."

"Here's a little something I like to do Tony Bennett style," Frank said. Then he relaxed his jaw and broke into the song "Too Young to Fall in Love."

"How about this Anthony Newley classic?" Frank said when he finished. Then he starts to sing "What Kind of Fool Am I?"

Adele hummed and swayed to the music. Her face was filled with light. Without her glasses her eyes looked pretty and deep blue. When Frank finished, she applauded wildly. It was as if she didn't even know I was there.

"Or how about this one?" Frank asked. "When I sing tonight, I'm going to leave them with this one."

I'll be loving you, always
With a love that's true, always . . .

"Oh, my God in heaven," Adele cooed. "That was the Irving Berlin song they played at my wedding."

Adele and Frank started in on the song in duet, and I stood there watching them, happy with their arms around each other's waists and not knowing what to do with myself except grin like I was enjoying being the third wheel. When Frank finished, he headed for the door.

"Break a leg," Adele called after him. "Frank's singing at a convalescent home picnic somewhere," Adele said, locking the door. Her face was aglow. "So. Tell me about the goings on in your life. What's new since I saw you last?"

That was exactly what I wanted Adele to tell me.

"It's nice you have a friend here," I said, trying to feel her out.

"Well, yes, but I wouldn't exactly say he's a friend. Frank sits across the table from me in the dining room. Sometimes I say, 'What's this?' and he'll tell me what's on my plate or maybe cut my food for me. But that's about the extent of it."

"Well, that sounds like a friend to me," I said. "He seems pretty young to be living here."

"Well, yes he is. He couldn't be more than sixty. He gets around. He can still come and go. Sometimes he doesn't even come home at all for supper. Last night I saved my cookie for him. Today was the first time he came in my room. He sings all right. Maybe Frank will take a liking to you," Adele said. "Of course I don't know if the kind of husband you're looking for is in a place like this."

"I'm not really looking," I told her. I didn't know if Adele was talking to me like a well-wishing grandmother or if she was just being a girl, fishing to find out if I liked the guy she really wanted. Either way, I was feeling uncomfortable.

"What was your husband's name?"

"Stanley," Adele said with conviction. "Stan."

"When you met Stan, was it love at first sight?"

"I think so," Adele said, being literal. "There were long intervals then when my eyesight worked okay. He used to come around my father's gas station. My father had a gasoline pump. In those days a pump was the size of a sewing machine. Stan was ten years older than me. Of course I was just an innocent."

"You mean you didn't start to learn about life before you moved away from home?"

"That's right," Adele said. "I'm sure at colleges and all it's nothing strange today for a boy to ask a girl out and maybe take her to the movies and then they fall into each other's arms. It must go on. But you didn't hear about it in my day."

"Those were just more private times."

"Well, yes, certainly," Adele said.

"Do you remember your wedding day?" I asked her.

"Sure." Adele smiled. "I was married in a synagogue. My best girl-friend was Catholic then. Her brother played the music during the ceremony and they sang that song, 'Not for just an hour, not for just a day, not for just a year, but always.' My husband wasn't Jewish but he converted. He was thirty-two when we married, and right before the ceremony he got circumcised."

"What?"

"It was just a formality."

"That's one hell of a formality," I said, trying not to sound sarcastic.

"Yes, but he always wanted to be circumcised," Adele defended herself. "He had to walk with a cane for a month."

"Sounds romantic," I said. "Were you happy on your wedding day?"

"Sure." Adele thought for a moment. "I guess so."

My heart opened. "I was miserable when I got married," I heard myself say. "It was the worst day of my life."

"Why?" Adele asked. "Because you couldn't wait to have a baby?"

"No, because I *was* one and I had married one. I knew I had made a mistake, but I didn't have the courage then to get out of it." I couldn't believe I was telling Adele this now when it had taken me years to admit it to even my closest friends.

"How old were you?" Adele asked kindly.

"Almost twenty-six."

"Oh, goodness," Adele said. Then she got silent. I felt completely ashamed. In Adele's eyes I was a loser now.

"We learn from our mistakes," Adele finally said.

"That's what I'm hoping for," I said. "It was in the seventies. We lived together first for almost three years."

"I don't believe in that living together stuff," Adele said.

"Everybody was doing it then," I explained. "It was supposed to be a way of trying out whether or not it would work."

"That didn't work," Adele deducted with ease. "I don't think your feelings for someone are the same when you live with them as when you marry them."

I had never heard anyone explain that problem so clearly.

"Well maybe next time you won't live with the person first," Adele said gently.

"I don't think I would. I'd get married or nothing. So far, it's been a lot of nothing."

"Why?" Adele asked. "Haven't you wanted another husband?"

"It's not that I haven't wanted a husband, I just haven't met anyone I wanted to spend that much time with, and I don't think I could handle another divorce."

"Why?" Adele wanted to know. "Was your first one very ugly?"

"Gargoylesque."

"Yup." Adele got quiet. "Those were the days. You'll grow. It will get better. You'll see. I was twenty-two when I got married. I was married forty years, and I don't think I'm inaccurate in saying most of that was my doing. My husband was attracted to women, and women were attracted to him. A lot of times when you're married you have to act like you're drunk even if you're not. Let's just leave it at that."

"I understand," I said.

"I wasn't the kind that could just turn off my love. Besides I had three small children to consider, which is good, because otherwise the years can go by and your husband dies before you, and believe me, without children, you can find yourself utterly alone."

"Has he been gone a long time?" I asked.

"He died in 1962," Adele said. Then she pointed to her arm. "Right here." It was the same spot on her shoulder where her daughter had died four years ago.

"Oh my God," I said.

"He was very sick."

"But you were so young."

"Yup," Adele said. "I was fifty-nine." Then she looked up to the ceiling.

"Did you ever think maybe you would find another man in your life?"

"Never," Adele said with great peace. "He was my one and only. He was charming and I was charmed. But I wish the best for you. I mean that sincerely. You still have time. It would be wonderful if you could fall in love again."

I smiled. Adele was my angel. She was my messenger of hope.

"If it's not too late, maybe you can still even have a child," Adele said. "We're not just here to dance through life, you know. We're here to make life."

"Well, I guess I missed the point." I could feel myself getting defensive. I never thought I would have a baby, but I never stopped hoping fate would intervene and show me I was wrong before it was too late.

"Now I'm too old, but here I am and I'm still alive," I said proudly. "I just must be here for another reason."

"Well, yes, probably." Adele thought it over. "You're barren."

IN WITH THE IN CROWD

It's not that I didn't have any kids in my life. The next Friday I had seven hundred of them in a grammar school assembly. I was a guest author talking to students as I had for ten years around the country, and today was the first time I had gone into a school since I adopted Adele. It felt good to be back with "my people" in the kindergarten through sixth grade. At one point in my presentation we would have a question and answer period. A kid would ask me how old I was, and somebody else might ask if I had pets or kids, or even if people stopped me for my autograph on the street. But nobody was going to accuse me of being barren.

Now I was talking to the kids about a book I wrote about a boy who was "too cool," and students were telling me cool was when you wore really "rad" clothes, or you had good hair or you were just popular. There was a cool girl clique on the right side of the room gossiping about a pocket of cool boys on the left, a nerd up front, and a sea of kids in the middle just trying to fit in. Today when I looked out at this young audience sitting shoulder to shoulder on the cafeteria floor, I thought of the Chit Chat Room and for a split second it was as if the school and the Chateau were one—a giant blur of prisoners. The difference here was when the bell rang, these kids had somewhere else they were going to go.

I thought of Adele sitting alone on the sofa, and a deep feeling of sadness and forgiveness came over me. I decided even though it wasn't my day, I would stop by and keep Adele company on my way home.

When I got to the Chateau, Adele was standing right outside the door poking her cane out on the step in front of her.

"I used to be able to walk by myself down to the tree and back," Adele told me. "Now I don't know if it's so wise. No one here so much as offers me a hand. They can see I'm standing here!"

Adele and I started for the tree just as a resident who looked mildly disconnected from his mind came out of the Chateau. "Who is she to you?" the man stopped me. "Are you her daughter?"

"I'm Adele's friend."

"Friend?" The man stormed away. "That's impossible! She doesn't have any friends."

"Oh, dear," Adele said. "I'm afraid there's some truth to that."

"I'm afraid that man is just missing cards from his deck," I said. I was hearing something I had never heard in my voice before. I was somebody's parent. And I was irate.

"You have friends," I said. "What about Frank?"

"Frank isn't talking to me at the table anymore," Adele said.

"Why not?" I asked.

"I don't know. All I could think is he doesn't like my voice because it's not as good as it used to be."

I could feel Adele's leg shaking. I was ready to barge back into the Chateau and demand an explanation from the principal why Adele wasn't being treated fairly. I asked Adele if she wanted to go to her room and get away from everybody, but she was fine going to the

Chit Chat Room. She said she could mentally run circles around these people, and besides it was almost time for the supper lineup.

"Let's just make the best of it," Adele said. She was a far more resilient old lady than I could ever hope to be. I decided to follow her advice and be strong. Back inside I recognized faces in the Chit Chat Room, and I tried to smile and say hello. There were three women playing cards at a table in the back. A woman was staring at the floor like this was the Museum of Electrical Sockets and she didn't want to miss viewing a single outlet. A man with a cane was about to start a fight with a man whose pants were slipping too low for my visual comfort. Even Vixen, the resident dog, was on the verge of collapse trying to work the room. So what did a person have to do to get a friend in this place?

"Adele wants to walk right up in your face," I overheard the warthog say, sitting on the sofa across from us with two other women. These were the popular ones.

"You can feel her breath," the woman on the sofa said beside her.

"I'm not equipped to handle that," the third one snipped. "Ask Phyllis when she comes. Even Phyllis couldn't talk to her."

My heart was hurting. I knew in that moment that most people never outgrow gossip. At least those women knew Adele's name. And who was this Phyllis person?

"This isn't much of a life," Adele told me.

"Then what is it?" I asked.

"It's not life when your own family doesn't want you. This is a place where you put people just to keep them out from under your feet."

I remembered the Adoption Manual guideline about keeping the adoptee from starting conversations that weren't upbeat. But Adele was feeling too much like a friend now not to hear her out.

"Phyllis is lucky," Adele said. "Her family always takes her out of here."

"Who is Phyllis?" I asked.

"She's one of the women who lives here. She has a wonderful family. They never leave her alone in here for long. The only time Phyllis doesn't like to stay out with them anymore is at night. Sometimes she's gone all day, and then she just comes back here at supper time."

Just then a pretty silver-haired woman came in on a walker. She had to be the one.

"How are you, Phyllis?" the warthog called.

"Not bad for an old broad." Phyllis laughed.

"Oh, you're not old," the second sofa woman said. "You look younger than any of us."

"She's older than I am," Adele tried to whisper.

"Who brought you back this time? Your daughter?" the warthog asked.

"No, my nephew today," Phyllis said. "Come on. It's time for dinner."

The warthog and the sofa women got up to walk with Phyllis. Phyllis saw me and stopped.

"Hello." She smiled. "Who's that?" Adele asked too loudly. "Phyllis?"

"Yes." Phyllis took a step back.

"Have you met Leah?" Adele asked.

"No, I haven't. But I've seen her here before. Are you from Braille?"

"No," I said.

"Are you some kind of volunteer?"

"I'm Adele's friend."

"Oh." Phyllis looked genuinely pleased. "That's nice." Her face was big and bright. She was nowhere close to Adele's age. Clearly this was just blindness and envy on Adele's part. I saw another aspect of Adele. Right now it made her seem almost cute.

"Leah is a very nice person," Adele said. "Of course, it's not the same thing as family."

"You're lucky to have such a good friend, Adele," Phyllis said. "I don't have any friends who visit me. Just my family."

"Yes, you're lucky," the sofa women said.

"I wonder if you wouldn't like my grandson." Phyllis looked right at me. "Yes. I think he would like you." Then she pinched my cheek and we all started walking. "He's a senior at USC."

"If I'm always staring at you, it's only because you're so pretty," the warthog said to me.

"You have very pretty hair," a sofa woman said. "Can I touch it?"

"Go ahead." I laughed. "It's real."

"My hair was all curls until I turned ninety," Adele offered. "Then it went flat as a pancake."

In the distance, I could see the lineup.

"You go ahead." The warthog winked at my taking Adele's arm. "You're young. I'm sure you have things you have to do. We'll walk together the rest of the way."

"Go!" Adele tried to order me. "Have a good time, you son of a gun. And whatever you do, drive carefully. Now that I found you, I don't want to lose you!"

Cool.

Memory Is a Miracle

A few days later, I was taking my daily walk at the neighborhood park where I had been going for years. I was talking to my park friend, Bob. Bob and I met on the track two years earlier, and we had been doing our laps there together pretty much every day since. I wasn't attracted to him, which was safe because he wasn't available anyway, but we could talk about almost anything. Today Bob was complaining about his girlfriend, and I was bragging about Adele.

"She's got incredible long- and short-term memory," I told him.

"That's really something for ninety-three," Bob said. "My memory isn't great now and I'm not even fifty. What's her secret? Find out. Does she take that Rocky Balboa?"

"You mean ginkgo biloba? The natural memory medicine?"

"Yeah, that's the stuff," Bob said. "I keep forgetting to buy a bottle."

*   *   *

The next day I went to be with Adele. I hoped I'd see her with the warthog and the sofa women, but I found her alone in her room.

"It's good to see you," she said. "Where are you?"

"I'm right here." I reached for her hand.

"Come here, you." Adele hugged me tight. She was in a good mood. "Come, sit with me. I was just thinking about an expression I have never thought of before. Memory bank. Have you heard of it?"

"I think so. What does it mean to you?"

"The memory stays in our bank from the time we're born until the time we die. I was just sitting here remembering things from the beginning of my life. Do you want to hear one of them?"

"Sure!"

"I can remember being just a few days old. I remember I knew 'I'm in this world now,' and I cried and cried. Preposterous sounding, isn't it?"

"Not to me, it isn't."

"Is it because I'm near the end of my life that all of this is converging from the beginning?"

"Do you feel like you're at the end of your life?"

"No," Adele said. "I don't think so. I don't feel like it. But I was remembering something from when I was three years old. My father came home from work, and my mother told him to hold me. I was crying, and he got disgusted and he threw me on the bed. It was a terrible shock. I remember it—the visual, in spite of being only three. I'm not used to talking to someone near this way that I'm talking to you."

"I understand," I said. But I didn't. My generation of women didn't know what it was like to not have other women you could really talk to. I felt honored that I was there now for Adele.

"These thoughts may not come again for quite a while," Adele said. "When you're in your nineties, you get nervous and you forget."

"You get like that in your forties, too."

"That's what my daughter tells me. And she's just in her sixties."

"I see that in schools with little kids," I told her. "They'll raise their hands. They're dying to be called on, and as soon as I pick them to speak they say, 'I forgot.'"

"Really?" Adele was astonished. "That young? Oh, I didn't forget *my* school. I remember I had to walk a scant block. It was on Waverly Avenue. One day the teacher suddenly discovered I had expression in my voice. That's when I started memorizing poetry. Recitation was high on entertainment in those days, you know. You don't know. You were too young."

"I wasn't born!"

Adele cleared her throat. Then she began:

> *Blessings on thee,* comma,
> *Little man,* comma.

"And you do not recite poetry in sing-song. If the next word goes into the next line, that's how you recite it."

> *Barefoot boy with cheeks of tan.* Period.
> *With thy turned up pantaloons,* comma
> *And thy merry* **whistled** [and you must say that with emphasis]
> *Tunes.*
> *Blessings on thee little man.*

"Oh, my God in heaven. And some say there's no memory bank!"

"That's amazing!" I said. "When was the last time you recited that?"

"I must have been eight years old," Adele said as if she was recalling the very day.

> *Under the spreading chestnut tree*
> *The village smithy stands;*

The smith, a mighty man is he,
With large and sinewy hands.

"Longfellow!" I was elated to remember. "I'm a poet, and I know it, my feet show it. They're Longfellow's! You recite that beautifully!"

"That was my mother's doing," Adele said proudly. "Others would have sing-sang the words, but not *my* mother. She wanted me to know every word. I wish you could have met her. She was a remarkable woman."

"She sounds like it from what you've told me."

"Did I tell you more than just a little? She was a business woman. Did I tell you this? She was the very first and only woman on the board of directors of what was the Atlantic & Pacific Tea Company. The A&P."

"Really? Good Lord!"

"Good Lord is right," Adele said. "She came up with the idea for buying in bulk with all those men. She sold shares of the company, and those stocks ended up being part of what was the very beginning of the stock market."

"That's incredible," I said. "She was really ahead of her time."

"Yes, she was. And do you want to know the most incredible part? She never left me alone one day. If she had to, my mother brought me with her, and I remember how I sat at that great big table with all those men."

"What did you do there?"

"My mother gave me paper and pencils to scribble with. She told me I wasn't to say a word, and I just did as I was told."

"That's really something. You did your first power meeting at eight."

"I'm sure I was younger than that." Adele laughed. "And at the end of the day, my mother would take me to Schraft's Candy Shop with the big counter and all sorts of chocolates. I could pick one out, or a lollipop. Those were the days."

"Sounds like it."

"Do you remember going to see your father at work?" I asked.

"No," Adele said. "He and my mother were totally different people. He was just a common laborer. For a long time my father worked in a factory that made the very fine hats for men, the Stetson hat. I do remember on Saturdays, though, when my father got his weekly pay, my mother and I would go down to meet my father at the local tavern. My father would give my mother the pay, and then he would stay and play cards with the men all afternoon and my mother and I would go to buy groceries. I remember how I would stand at my father's chair while he was sleeping in it." Adele giggled. "I would stand there with a comb and part his hair down the middle. Then I'd comb it all to the side and laugh because of all the times I did that, he never once woke up! Can you imagine?"

I tried to imagine how Adele's mother and father might have gotten along with her being so strong at that time. I tried to call up a clear, poignant memory of my childhood with my mother and father, but in that moment I couldn't. "I have memories of my parents," I said, "but the memory doesn't feel like a reality in my life like yours do now."

"Sure." Adele smiled. "That's why those are what are called the good old days, but you'll see when you get older."

I'll see what? I felt annoyed, like I was a kid being left out of some great secret.

"It all comes back. Sure." Adele's voice got excited. "You sit and your mind backs up on you, and everything comes before you again and it's completely vivid."

"Does that mean when I'm ninety I'll finally remember what I did with my black silk skirt I misplaced when I was forty?"

"Could be," Adele said knowingly.

"But what good is it going to do me when I'm ninety? I won't be able to fit into the skirt!"

"You'll see," Adele said. "The memory bank. It's quite the mystery. Memory is a miracle. Don't you think?"

Right now memory seemed very overrated.

"Miracle or a practical joke."

"Oh, it's a miracle. It's all I've got!"

Teeth and Other Things That Come Out at Night

"She's unbelievable," I told Bob about Adele out on the track the next day. "She's lucid and passionate, and she's left for dying in that place. But she's totally alive. She could be the poet laureate. She still has plenty to give. Do you know how few people there are in this country who are as old as she is? She was born in 1903! That was the year the Wright brothers flew their first airplane!"

"Wow." Bob got it. "That's not an old lady, that's a paratrooper."

The next Saturday when I went to see Adele, she came to her door with her finger in her mouth.

"I was thinking maybe I should get my teeth fixed," Adele said as she let me in.

"What's the matter with them?"

"They hurt, then they don't hurt," Adele complained.

All I wanted to know was if they were good enough to chew. In an hour it would be time for lunch. "Do they do the trick?" I asked her.

"Sure." Adele smiled. Then she made her lower plate come out with her tongue like she was opening and closing a drawer. "I can do the same with the uppers," Adele offered. She repositioned her tongue.

"That's okay." I laughed. I was caught completely off guard. I was watching a teenager playing with her dentures, and I was trying hard not to encourage her. This was serious.

"Did you tell anybody you're in pain?" I asked.

"You could be in your room all day and die at night, and nobody would know it," Adele said without hesitation. That was not the answer I wanted to hear.

"Would it help if you had a telephone in this room?"

"Maybe," Adele said, "but it costs extra. Besides, who am I going to call? I can't see the numbers to dial."

"I see you have the intercom button on the wall." I could feel myself straining to be helpful. "You can always push that button for help, right?"

"Well, yes." Adele seemed flustered. "But they say that's just for emergencies."

"Your tooth hurts and you pay for these people here to help you," I said. "So what constitutes an emergency?"

"I don't know," Adele said. "I've only used it once. When my old roommate Sally was having a stroke."

I suggested we take a walk down to the front desk and see if someone there couldn't make a dental appointment for Adele.

"All right," Adele said. "Of course, I did just go to the dentist a few weeks ago. What if the dentist doesn't want to see me again this soon?"

Adele and I started down the hall. I was trying hard to have patience with her, but she was turning into everything I didn't want an old lady to be: someone who thought like an old person. I had to remind myself that Adele was from the generation of women who didn't ever ask for a second opinion because they didn't want to hurt the first doctor's feelings. She had no way of knowing that in today's world if her dentist needed to make a boat payment, he would be happy to see her again.

"Of course, I suppose if something were to happen to me," Adele said, "and you or my family didn't just happen to be here at the moment that it happened, and I had a new roommate, I suppose she could go fetch the doctor or someone without having to press the emergency buzzer."

"That's true," I said.

"But if I ever *do* get a roommate," Adele said halfway down the hall, "she'll have to know I get up a half dozen times in the night to urinate. That's what happens when you get to be ninety."

"Ninety? That's what happens to me now." I tried to clue her in.

"You're kidding?" Adele said. "At your age?"

"Yes," I tried to say without sounding like I was talking to a person who just crawled out from under a rock. Had she never heard of PMS, or didn't she remember perimenopause or the dreaded change?

"I use diapers," Adele said too loudly. "They have a free box for you here in your room when you first move in. You just put them on like a pair of big plastic underpants." Adele stopped to show me with her hands the size of the things. I didn't want to look. You couldn't call for emergency help in this place unless you had a Code Blue, but diapers were on the house. I prayed God would save me in the end from this final indignity.

"I mean I put one on, but I don't have to actually use it," Adele went on, perfectly at ease. "I've worn the same one for weeks. I still have lots in my room. Have you tried them?"

"Not yet."

When we got to the front desk, Adele called out to speak to the administrator, Joanna.

"Didn't you just see the dentist last week?" Joanna leaned over the desk and spoke straight into Adele's face.

"Well, yes," Adele said.

"And did the dentist tell you to make an appointment?" she asked like she was talking to a ten-year-old.

"No," Adele said. "But my teeth are hurting!"

Adele was the voice of sanity and reason, and I was proud.

"Oh. Well then, I'll call." Joanna stepped back. She was clearly embarrassed. "But you may have to wait a day before the dentist can see you."

Adele and I started back for her room. "So I'll wait a day." Adele stuck her finger in her mouth like it was no big deal. "They don't hurt if I don't play with them," Adele said.

"So then don't play with them!" I said.

"Easy for you to say." Adele laughed. "What else am I going to play with at *my* age?"

The New Roommate

A few days later I was at an annual girls-only dinner party at my friend Barb's house in the Hollywood Hills. When Barb's friend Annette saw me, her jaw just about hit the table.

"You look younger than you did last year," she said, loud enough for everyone to hear. "You're positively glowing. What's going on? Are you seeing somebody?"

"Yeah," I said, trying not to blush. "She's ninety-three!" I joked that the secret to looking and feeling younger was to hang out with a woman ninety or over, and everybody wanted to know more. The truth was that the more time I spent with Adele, the more at peace I felt with myself. But I was not less afraid of getting old.

Annette didn't want to hear about it. "Getting old isn't that bad." She laughed.

Of course it wasn't. Annette had already had her eyes fixed, and she was scheduled to have her cheeks hoisted the next month.

"I think you just don't ever want to be old and alone," Annette said. "We've got to find Leah a decent husband before it's too late." Annette put out the alarm.

"What's too late?"

"The longer you live by yourself, the harder it's ever going to be to give up your freedom to let somebody in your space. Recall getting married and having that new roommate in your twenties?" Annette tried to take me through an imaging process. "Now picture the difference between that and how much you're going to enjoy it if you have to pick up some guy's socks off the floor for the first time when you're fifty. The shock alone could kill you!"

The other women laughed. I felt mildly ill.

*   *   *

Wednesday something told me I should drop by the Chateau for a quick visit with Adele. When I got there, I found her standing at the front desk. Her voice sounded too soft and shaky. She was asking the girl on duty why Dr. Campbell, the Chateau doctor, wouldn't prescribe something to settle her nerves, and all the girl kept saying was "You don't need that, honey." When I told Adele I was there, she reached out for my hands and she wouldn't let them go.

"Just when I need someone to help me, you're here," Adele said, almost in tears.

"Is something wrong?" I asked.

"Something terrible has happened," Adele said, trying to collect herself. "Come. I'll show you. I got a roommate!"

We started slowly down the hallway for her room. "Oh, my God in heaven," Adele said. "It's a good thing we can't see what's coming ahead of us."

Adele could say that again. The new roommate had her own queen-sized bed with a gigantic teddy bear on it and a huge television on her own dresser—one larger than Adele's dresser, which came with the room. Now in order to fit everything in, they had to rearrange Adele's bed and chair on an angle so that the room looked like a furniture warehouse or the scene of a very bad, old Helen Keller joke. The most upsetting sight of all was the counter where Adele liked to keep her tape recorder and talking books. It was now covered by a small black refrigerator.

"Where are your talking books?"

"They put them under here someplace." Adele felt frantically around the counter. "But I can't see them. There's no room left for me here, anywhere. I hope nothing like this ever happens to you. And I mean that sincerely. Oh, God. Give me strength."

Just then the door opened, and a small bony woman came in on a walker. She had the face of an old sea captain, and her mouth was closed and moving round and round so she looked like she was chewing on a wad of tobacco.

"Is someone there?" Adele called. "Lorraine? Is that you?"

"Mm hmm," Lorraine answered.

"Lorraine, I'd like you to meet my friend Leah," Adele said.

"Mm hmm," Lorraine answered.

"Leah's a writer," Adele said. "She has a little bit of a mind."

"Mm hmm," Lorraine said. Then she climbed into bed.

This was it. This was Adele's forever. At ninety-three, at an age when a change in laundry detergent could rattle the nerves to the root, Adele was supposed to adapt to this. I didn't know how she'd survive.

"It's just that it came without warning," Adele said. "My talking books are all I have in here. Why does she even need an icebox, anyway? We eat at five-thirty."

I didn't know, but I would find out. Somebody had to be in Adele's corner like Lorraine's family obviously was for her. Walking down to the counter alone that day it felt good to know that the only somebody could be me. But when I went to the front desk, I found out Lorraine had nobody in her corner. She had no family. Lorraine had been moved there by the state.

Two days later I couldn't stay away from the Chateau. I had to make sure Adele was all right. When I got to her room, the refrigerator was gone. The tape player and Adele's talking books were back on the counter. Adele was listening to *The Teachings of Blaise Pascal* loud, and Lorraine was in bed watching *Geraldo*. Beside Lorraine on the floor was the bear, a carton of Marlboros, peanut butter, and an open packet of saltines. A sock was halfway across the border to Adele's side of the room. There was a tinge of urine in the air. This was no longer Adele's room. This was no longer to be our sanctuary away from the Chit Chat Room. This was the regular world now, and I didn't know how I was going to make it in there in the long term.

Just then there was a knock on the door, and a woman came in wearing a babushka and a shirtwaist from the old country. She lifted her fingers to her mouth as if she was taking a drag off a cigarette. Lorraine nodded to the woman. Then she got out of bed.

A few seconds later a man on a cane came to the door and did the same thing. Lorraine headed for the door. One thing was obvious: the older you got, the less cool it looked to smoke.

"All she does all day is sit in bed or go out for a smoke," Adele told me. "Those people come by day and night to bum cigarettes. Then I listen to her coughing all night. It sounds horrible."

"Does she always have the TV on?" I asked.

"Not always. But enough so that I have to turn up the talking machine. It's not like she and I have anything to talk about. There's absolutely no conversation. I might as well be living with a corpse. She doesn't utter a word unless I ask her. Half the time I don't even know when she's here. I ask her just to tell me when she's leaving. How difficult is it to say, 'I'm leaving?'"

At that moment, it seemed impossible. But there was nothing I wanted to say more. Being there was excruciating.

"Can you imagine?" I asked Bob out on the track that evening. "To be in your nineties and all of a sudden to be expected to live with a stranger?"

"No," Bob said. Bob had been divorced as long as I had. We laughed like an old couple who understood. He was having a hard time just making it through living at his girlfriend's on the weekends. "I'm too much of a coward," Bob said. "I could never live like Adele. I could only do it if I had rope."

"Why a rope?" I asked.

"To hang myself."

*   *   *

The next day I went to Adele's for my regular Saturday visit. She wasn't waiting for me in the Chit Chat Room. I went down to her room, but when I knocked there wasn't an answer. I didn't hear a sound and I feared the worst. Adele was dead.

I went down to the front desk just as Joanna told me she was on her way to Adele's room. An ambulance had been called, and the driver was waiting outside. Joanna was at least fifteen years younger than me, and she seemed relaxed, as if she was used to seeing this on a regular basis. I stood behind her while she unlocked the door.

"Come on, Lorraine, honey," Joanna called into the room.

Lorraine was sitting on her bed. Adele was sitting in the chair beside her.

"Who's there?" Adele asked.

"It's me, Joanna," the girl said. "Lorraine, honey, time to go. The ambulance is here."

"Try not to be afraid," Adele said sweetly. She reached for Lorraine's hand. "We've lived through harder than this. They'll take some tests. You'll probably be back home tomorrow."

"Mm hmm," Lorraine said.

"I'll save you my fudge brownie from the Seniors' Center," Adele said. "I'll just wrap it up. It's perfectly good. You'll enjoy that."

"Okay," Lorraine answered. "Thank you." Then she went with Joanna to the door. I sat down in the rocker beside Adele. It was quiet in there again.

"You were very kind to Lorraine," I said.

"I was just lending a helping hand," Adele said modestly.

"I bet it will feel good to have your room back to yourself if only for a day."

"I hope that's all it is," Adele said.

"What do you mean?"

"I don't mind telling you I don't relish the loneliness. The older you get it's better just to have another live body around than to be alone. Especially at night. Do you know what I mean?"

"Sure I do." I just didn't know what I was supposed to do to make it happen.

I drove off to the park. It was earlier than my regular evening walking time with Bob, but I needed to move and I hoped I'd see him there. I wasn't in the mood to walk alone. I started to think. What kind of a rest of my life was I going to have? Was I going to be seventy and still just walking around that track every day with Bob? Was that all there was?

Something had to give.

REMEMBERING SEX

Four days later, Lorraine still was not back from the hospital. I found Adele alone on a sofa in the Chit Chat Room. When I asked her what news she had heard about Lorraine, Adele laughed.

"They don't tell you anything about anything around here," she said. "Maybe they think I'm still not old enough to know the facts of life. If I was Lorraine's family, that would be another story. Of course everything would be a different story if I had a family that wanted me."

Adele was slipping into darkness, and I had to find a way fast to keep her out of there. Then I saw the savior. It was a flier on the wall. It said: COME TO THE CALIFORNIA CHATEAU'S GREAT WESTERN FAMILY BBQ. It had a drawing on it of an old, fat cowboy with big jowls and no teeth sitting alone at a bar. This was an invite to fun. It seemed like a long shot, but I had to try.

"Hey, Adele," I said. "Look! There's going to be a party here Saturday night, and you're invited."

"Really?" Adele's voice lifted. "With dancing? Can I wear what I have on now or maybe something more fancy?"

I was taken aback. I hadn't seen anybody get so genuinely excited about a party where there wasn't going to be alcohol since I was a little girl. I looked around, a little bit embarrassed that Adele was too happy and making a scene. Then I couldn't deny that I felt excited, too. I asked Adele if she wanted me to help her pick something fancy from her closet. Then we headed down the hallway. I couldn't remember the last time I had helped a girlfriend get dressed for a party.

"I know for a fact, if there's anything we know for a fact, I think I could still go to town with a man," Adele said.

"I bet you could."

"Sure. When I hear music, I want to dance. Or when I get dressed to look nice, I'll put on black shoes instead of tan, that's all part of the sex attraction. I mean I don't know if it's the real sexual desire I still feel, but something is still there. It's surprising that it's there, but it is."

"Sure it is," I said. "Your sex is who you are. You give me hope. They say women supposedly peak sexually in their forties and men in their twenties."

"Horse feathers." Adele unlocked her door. "Men are ready all the time. Sex alone isn't everything as you get older, anyway. You've got to really have the desire to go through it and enjoy it."

"That's for sure," I said.

"And there has to be a lot of humor and compassion because if your body is all you've got to take into the bedroom with you, you may be sunk."

"And how," I concurred. I felt awkward letting this conversation go on with a ninety-year-old woman. Didn't anyone tell her she was ninety? I looked over at Adele. No matter how old a person is, everyone remembers making love. I just hoped Adele wouldn't say something over the edge.

"I shouldn't say this," Adele said, "because it's only talk, you know, but I could go through the whole act as if it mattered."

"Well, we're women." I didn't know what else to say. "We're trained to fake a lot. Did you fake it with your husband?"

"I don't know if it was a lot," Adele said. "I liked sex. But you know that my husband was attracted to women. We'll just leave it at that."

"Well, thank God we're not in India," I heard myself say. "They would have cut out our clitorides to make sure we never had any pleasure—faked or otherwise."

"Well, yes," Adele said, like that was to be understood. "Really?"

"Really. Did your mother ever talk to you about sex?"

"I was sent to my girlfriend's the night before my sister was born," Adele said. "I wasn't allowed to know. Kids didn't know. That stuff wasn't discussed. And in those days, women didn't have their babies in a hospital. Or very few did. So it was all happening in the home. I don't even think I knew my mother was pregnant. She still went to work. That's how much we talked about sex. And it's funny the things that stick out in your memory, and then we completely forget about them until years later."

"Like what?"

"Well, like when I was ten years old, the same year my sister was born, my father's cousin stayed with us. He was a sailor and he was off duty. And once, when my mother and father weren't around, he lifted me up by my elbows so high that his face was right up even with where it shouldn't have been, and he shook his head back and forth right there."

A chill ran through my body. "I'm so sorry that happened to you."

"Well, you know, I was only ten. The memory wasn't too painful emotionally. But then he came back again when I was twelve. That was another story. He told me, 'Don't ever tell anyone what you saw with me.' And from that time on, I started to lose my sight. My parents thought it was because I got silver polish in my eyes, and they took me to the best doctor who thought the same thing, but I wonder."

"And over the years you never remembered that again?"

"Once in a while the feeling came back where he lifted me. But I never remembered the incident until I started these talks with you a few days ago. Isn't that amazing how the memory bank works?"

"It sure is." I wanted to cry. "They put people in jail for acts like that now. It's called sexual abuse. I'm sure it's gone on since the beginning of time."

"Well, of course." Adele held my hand so as to comfort me. Then her voice got excited again. "So tell me all the details of the party. And read slowly. Did it say the party was for family?"

"That's what it says."

"Will you be my family?"

"I'd be honored to be your family." I felt my insides beaming.

"Those who are, aren't."

"Now, now. I'd be happy to come. The flier says there will be lots of good food, some drink, and songs that will remind you of when you were 'in the pink.'"

"I'm still in the pink," Adele said matter-of-factly.

"I know that. You're in the bright pink."

"I'm glad somebody thinks so," Adele said. "Come on. Help me pick out something to wear. And no pantaloons!"

We went through Adele's closet, and she slowly felt all the safety pins on the clothes to see which were the black pants and which blouse was red. Then we got her tan shoes down out of their box. When we got done, I needed a nap. I had a date that night.

"I'd better get going," I said.

"Well, do you have to?"

"I've got to go get ready. I'm going out tonight with a boy."

"Is he old enough?"

"I think so, but I'm not a hundred percent convinced. Chronologically he's forty-three, but he's an actor. We're going to some big studio party for the opening of a movie."

Adele wasn't the least bit impressed about the party. "Is this actor someone serious?" she wanted to know. "Should I be happy for you?"

"If you'd like, but this is our fourth date. I wouldn't go out and buy a dress or anything."

"Well, of course not, smarty pants. Not just after a fourth date. But have a good time and don't do anything I wouldn't do."

"And what might that be?"

Adele smirked and folded her hands. "Let's not get into that."

THE CALIFORNIA CHATEAU GREAT WESTERN FAMILY BARBECUE

I was home trying to figure out what to wear for my date that night when Jenny called me from her car phone. Jenny's business was high fashion and she accessorized the stars, but when it came to going to a Hollywood party, Jenny's outfit of choice was a ripped T-shirt she could wear while she was in bed reading murder mysteries.

"Can't you just get out of it?" Jenny asked. "That's why I ask everyone I know to please not invite me to their parties anymore because I just have to make up some lie of an excuse why I'm not going to be there. Is that actor that great?"

Two hours later I was standing at the gala opening party for the movie with my date, the actor. It was just him and me and a thousand other people and the crew from *Entertainment Tonight* taping stars walking down the red carpet. I felt lonely and I was daydreaming about Saturday. I kept picturing myself walking into the Chateau Family Barbecue with Adele on my arm. I had a feeling it was going to be the most entertaining party I had been to in years. On the one hand, I prayed that I was right. On the other, I feared that if I was, I would never want to party with my peers again.

*   *   *

Come Saturday, I was just excited. I could tell Adele was excited too because I heard her singing "Home on the Range" from outside the Chateau, and the party hadn't even started yet. When I stepped into the Chit Chat Room to find her, I saw something that threw me. Adele was all dressed up sitting on the sofa, and this time she was not alone. A woman was sitting beside her. I had never seen this woman before, but it was obvious she and Adele were becoming fast friends. When Adele realized I was there, she started to work me like I was a bad date.

"I couldn't remember if this party was just for the inmates." She laughed too loud. I reminded Adele it was for the "inmates" and their families, and today I was her family. Remember?

"Of course I remember." Adele smiled. "I just didn't know if you would remember." Then she tried to whisper, "You don't mind if Mary here comes with us, do you? She doesn't have anybody."

"Not at all!" Mary's and my eyes met. In that instant I knew no matter how many years you've lived, nobody was ever old enough to go to a party alone.

Now it was almost Saturday night, and we were three single girls starting down the hall to the party. Of the three of us, Mary was the prettiest: Scandinavian with gray-white hair and dim blue eyes. She was also the least mentally stacked. We had to keep telling her, when she asked us every ten seconds, that she shouldn't just go back to her room and that we really wanted her to come with us. Really.

"That's what you get for being a good person," Adele said.

"Be careful. You'll give me a swollen head," Mary said sweetly.

History told me I had definitely been to this party before. Later on, Mary would be the one of us who went back to her room with the only available dreamboat of the night, and Adele and I would kick ourselves for letting her tag along in the first place.

" 'Home, home on the range,' " Adele sang. " 'Where the deer and the antelope play.' I've got a hankering for some good jolly music. I hope it's not the artificial stuff. Let's hurry!"

I was with a young girl wanting to run ahead. She didn't know I hadn't hurried to show up early to a party since I was sweet sixteen. Nobody had taught Adele modern party protocol.

When we walked into the party it was obvious that unless you came in a wheelchair, all that being fashionably late here meant was that you wouldn't get a place to sit but you may get in a fight. Adele's regular table was free but her chair wasn't. An old Russian man was reserving it for his son the doctor who promised he was coming, and there was no way the man was going to let the chair go. "Even if she *is* blind."

The band started to play, and Adele wanted to know whether we were facing the music and if it was artificial. It was "Ben and Mitsy Parker" and their artificial music machine.

"Wonderful!" Adele said, clapping her hands with delight. "It's real people."

> *Hello, ma baby*
> *Hello, ma honey*
> *Hello, my ragtime gal*

"I used to be a soprano," Adele told me. "Then, of course, you know, when I hit ninety, my voice fell into the basement. Sing the next one with me." I looked around to see if anyone was watching.

> *Ta-ra-ra-Boom-de-ay!*
> *Ta-ra-ra-Boom-de-ay*
> *Ta-ra-ra-Boom-de-ay*
> *Ta-ra-ra-Boom-de-ay*

"This is ridiculous," a man sitting next to Adele called out. "I'm waiting an hour already just for something to eat. I could have gone to Coney Island and back for a hot dog. All this noise and energy is driving me crazy."

"Is there a good turnout?" Adele asked, squeezing my hand. "You be my eyes. Do people look like they're enjoying themselves?"

I told Adele they had fixed up the dining room with balloons and cut-out horses and that there were more people here than I had ever seen. What I didn't tell her was that most of them looked either distraught or dead. And that was just the families—the children of the residents.

I had been with these children somewhere before. It was in high school. We were stuck at a barbecue with our parents and a roomful of their really old friends. Now I tried to smile at the Russian man's son, who had shown up but who wanted nothing to do with any of this. This was a place to get in and out of fast. He tied a Power Rangers bib around his father. Side by side, they looked like a before and after picture.

"It's nice to see some of these people not just sitting like a bump on a log for once in a year, don't you think?" Adele said, clapping to the music.

A staff person came through pushing a cart with little cups of medicine on it. Adele was one of her stops. "Here you go, Adele," she said. I had never seen Adele being medicated, but it felt like it had to be a mistake. They were trying to spike the wrong girl. Somebody had to tell them Adele was the only one there who didn't need to get high. She was already there.

Adele took the cup and swallowed the pills like it was a shot of tequila. "I'd like to take a few steps on the dance floor," she said to me. "But I don't want people to think I look like a fool."

"Don't be afraid to look like a fool." I heard those words come out of my mouth as if I knew what I was talking about. "We should just take a walk out there and all look like fools together. We're all old enough to have nothing to lose. We can go out there and have some fun."

Mary tried to back out, but I told her there was no way.

"We all stick together, and no one leaves with a boy unless the other two know," I said. "Okay?"

"Okay." Mary giggled. "You're in charge. Whatever you say goes." That's how it seemed. I had never felt so powerful at a party. Adele felt for my arm, and we headed up to the floor. Ben and Mitsy played:

Oh, you beautiful doll.
You great big beautiful doll.

Mary took my other hand and did the shimmy, and Adele tried to walk to the beat. Nobody was on the dance floor. Nobody had been on it once. We were just three girls who wanted to get closer to the band. Adele tapped her foot to the music. Then before I could stop her, she dropped her purse to the floor and started to dance. Mary joined in doing her own free-form hip swivel, and I was just standing there. I was afraid Adele was going to lose her balance so I reached out to hold her, but before I could, Adele grabbed my hands and turned me into her dance partner.

She was leading me in what I thought was the fox-trot. All I knew for certain was we were going too fast. Mary did something like the mashed potato off to the side of the dance floor, and now it was just Adele and me and Ben and Mitsy Parker. I had never been here before. I had never been part of the only couple on the dance floor—the couple that everybody was talking about.

"I feel sorry for her," I heard someone say. "What could be worse than being blind?"

I looked at Adele. Her face was wild and laughing. "You've got the wrong foot," she said.

"I don't know how to dance like this," I tried to say loudly over the music. "You'll have to give me some lessons."

"Oh, for goodness' sake," Adele said. "Didn't any man ever teach you to dance? Just follow me. And see what you can do about staying off my toes."

I held on tight to Adele, and she twirled me around. I knew the band was playing something fast, but I didn't hear the music. I was with my father, dancing at my wedding. I was at the Springsteen concert, and Bruce had just picked me from the crowd to come and dance with him on stage.

> *You can't start a fire*
> *Worrying about your little world falling apart,*
> *This gun's for hire.*
> *Even if we're just dancing in the dark.*

I was with the oldest and blindest person in the room, and I was so incredibly proud. I wanted everyone to see she was alive and worth knowing. This was the dance of my life.

"That's enough for right now," Adele said when the song stopped. "Not bad for ninety-four, huh?"

"You're remarkable."

"Tell that to my family." Adele caught her breath.

"I am your family. Remember?"

"Oh, right," Adele said, checking her talking watch. It was ten minutes to six. In ten minutes the party would be over. This was the first party I had been to since the third grade that lasted two hours only, and it was the first time I could remember being at a party where I stayed from beginning to end. In a few moments I would go home and put my heating pad on my back.

"You know what I think when I dance like that?" Adele said. "The expression 'God gives with one hand and takes away with the other.'"

"Well, he sure has given you a lot," I said.

"I guess he has," Adele said. "I'm glad you came with me to this get-together."

"I'll go with you anytime," I said. "I hope you won't take this the wrong way, but I love you. And I mean it."

"I like you a little." Adele laughed. "You're my kind of gal."

A Class on
Current Events

I left the Chateau buzzing. It's not that I hadn't had enough partying for one day, but two hours later I was figuring out how soon I could go back. I knew Monday morning was the Chateau current events class and that Adele didn't miss one of them. Current events sounded intriguing to me. I decided Monday morning I would surprise Adele and show up. Having me there would make her day.

Sunday night I was lying in bed mulling over the definition of current events at the Chateau. I figured the class would have to be a toned-down version of the late night news since nobody Adele's age needed to be subjected to that full-blown insanity. At 3:30 I was trying to fall asleep, knowing the concern and excitement I was experiencing was just what any average, overly anxious parent felt the night before she dropped in on her child in class unannounced. I knew hanging out so much with Adele was probably not socially healthy, but I couldn't deny it was old people who were bringing me back to life. I just wasn't ready to admit it yet, either.

Monday morning I almost couldn't get to the Chateau because there was an early morning bank robbery at the local Bank of America. The streets were blocked and barricaded. A police helicopter was hovering low enough to blow out your eardrums, and yet one step inside the Chateau was like entering a safe, secret society where they had no idea what danger was going on outside. They had problems of their own in there. A monthly residents gripe session was wrapping up in the Chit Chat Room. The warthog was at the podium.

"Who else?" she barked. "Speak now or forever hold your peace."

"There's a woman who keeps walking past my door in the middle of the night," a man complained. "So I had to hit her. And if anybody finds a dead person, I didn't mean to kill her." People nodded. Another night, another murder.

There was a group of people waiting together for the current events class to begin. I saw Adele sitting alone on a sofa. I sat down beside her quietly and I reached for her hand.

Adele was neither surprised nor delighted to find out I was there. When I tried to reminisce about our dance together on Saturday night, it was as if Saturday never existed. I was ready to go home. I was afraid that in the last forty-eight hours Adele's short-term memory had taken an abrupt slip downward.

"Did something happen?" I asked her. "Do you feel all right?"

"I feel unhappy," Adele said without missing a beat.

"Oh." I was not used to somebody being so current to their feelings and then not apologizing for it afterward.

"I'm so terribly lonely in my life," Adele went on. "I've always had people, but here I have absolutely nobody. No one wants to lend a kind word or a helping hand or even talk to me."

"Have you tried talking to them?" I asked.

"I try to say 'good morning' now and then, but it's no use," Adele said.

"Well, what about your new friend Mary?" I asked. "Where is she?"

"She never comes to this class," Adele said sadly. "As soon as she heard that it was going to start, she left me here and went down to her room. She said she doesn't want to know about the news. Mary is a very sweet person, but I think there's something ever so slightly tainted about her. But you'll really like Polly." Adele's voice perked up. "Polly teaches this class. Polly makes life worth living in this place if I can go that far. She calls things as she sees them, good or bad. Just like the way life is. And right now, life stinks."

An attractive woman in her late sixties came into the room carrying a handful of newspaper clippings. I prayed the news would be good.

"What's happening in the world?" Polly asked. "Who can tell me: What day is this?"

"Monday," some of the residents answered.

"Good," Polly said. "And where do we live?"

"Los Angeles," some other residents chimed in.

"That's right," Polly said. "In what state?"

"Colorado."

"No," some other residents said. "California."

"That's right," Polly said. "We live in California. And who can tell me what's the weather like today?"

"Cool," a woman answered.

Yes, this was. This was like a kindergarten class. This was all of the news these people needed to know. This was the safe and accurate news from a simpler, kinder America these people once knew. This was the news of the idealistic America of the sixties when I was in Mrs. Liebling's class and we started each day with our hand on our hearts saying, "I pledge allegiance to the flag . . ." I could relax. Everything was going to be fine.

"Mike Tyson fought Evander Holyfield Saturday night in Vegas,"

Johnny (the Hawaiian-chicken-hula man) called out. "Did you see that? He won thirty million bucks!"

"That's not the important news," the warthog snapped. "Mike Tyson is an animal. He bit that man's ear off."

"Yes, that was pretty ridiculous, wasn't it?" Polly asked.

"We had a dog named Frosty who lived to be nineteen," a woman with two teeth called out. "Do you know why he lived so long? He ate chicken noodle soup. The vet couldn't believe it! He never saw a poodle that old!"

"I've got to find my wife," a man called. "I woke up and she just wasn't there. What day is it?"

"I saw a picture of President Clinton," a woman named Nora said. "He looked so old. He's not going to last long."

"How long do you think you'd last if you were president?" Johnny asked.

"I don't think presidents should have sex," Nora said. "Look at that Paula Jones thing. That woman's trying to sue him for sexual harassment."

"What's that?" a woman asked.

"She wants two million dollars," Phyllis called out. "Can you believe it?"

"Why?" another woman asked. "Did he open her up?"

I wanted to cover Adele's ears, but I wasn't sure if she was listening anyway. What could two million dollars for making a pass at someone sound like to a woman who earned twenty thousand dollars in her lifetime?

"Who wants to be president?" Polly asked. "They dig up all the dirt on you. Every mistake you ever made."

"The longer you live, you know you are your mistakes," Phyllis said.

"The perfect person is an angel," Adele mumbled. "And I'm not ready to be an angel yet."

That was good news to me.

"I saw the girl last night on the TV who tossed her baby into a Dumpster," Nora said. "It made me so mad because I couldn't have a baby."

Nora started to weep. She was a big woman in a faded sleeveless dress. All I could do was look at the tops of her arms shaking. I had never seen anyone that old cry like that before. Apparently the pain never stopped and it never went away.

"These are the sad times that are hard to remember when we look back on our lives," Polly said sweetly. A woman next to Nora gently touched Nora's hand like one of my girlfriends might do for me.

"Yup," Adele said to herself softly. Her hands were folded across her lap. "We've seen it all."

Then Polly opened one of her newspapers and began to read.

"I found this article in the *Times* on colds. It says people who are more social catch fewer colds."

"You would think it would be the opposite," Phyllis said.

"Yes, you would," Polly agreed. "That you'd pick up people's bacteria, but what this research says is that loners are four times more likely to come down with colds than people who have friends or family or even coworkers. That suggests that the more you reach out, the happier you are. Happiness boosts your immune system."

"I suppose that's right," Adele mumbled.

"When was the last time you had a cold?" I asked her.

"Oh, I don't know," Adele said. "Years."

"You're lucky," I said to her. "You're strong as a horse and healthy as an ox."

"Am I anything like a human?" Adele asked.

"Absolutely."

"Well, then I don't want to get sick now." She lifted her head proudly. "Who will I have to take care of me?" Adele suddenly spoke out. "Putting out a helping hand gives one satisfaction."

"That's right, Adele." Polly smiled. Then she walked over to our sofa. "It's good to hear you today, Adele," she said. "I see you brought a young friend with you."

"Yes," Adele said too loudly. "I think to have a friend you must be a friend. You can't just expect everybody to come to you."

"I would agree with you, Adele," Polly said.

"Of course, extending a hand to others is not new to me," Adele called out. "I used to volunteer for the Red Cross. I wish I could still go out and do for others. My whole life I always did for others."

"You can do for others right here, Adele," Polly said. "Would you please lead us in our closing song?"

Adele's face filled with light.

Phyllis went to the piano and started to play the introduction. Then everyone became silent and sat up straight. With Adele leading the way they sang "God Bless America." They sang that song like I had never heard it before. They understood each word and they sang it proud.

"We sang this when America was young," Adele said to me. "We always sing it at the end of the class after we talk about what's happening in the news. Don't you remember it?"

I was having a hard time remembering. The words to "God Bless America" sounded like news to me now. I hoped I could still be young enough in my day to feel the words.

THE SING-ALONG

"Hey, Bob," I said the next day after our third mile out on the track. "Want to play a game for the next lap?"

"Sure," he said. "What's the prize?"

"The prize is I name a song, and you see if you can sing all the words."

"Now there's a lotto win for you." Bob laughed so I could see he had front teeth like a crocodile. "I can't carry a tune, my voice cracks, and I sing completely out of time. So you have to give me a quarter for every song I get right. Deal?"

"You're on. Song number one: 'God Bless America.'"

"Are you kidding?" Bob tried to laugh. Then he cleared his throat.

> *God bless America*
> *Land that I love.*
> *Stand beside her, and guide her . . .*
> *Da de da—la—dee dee, dum-dee dum.*

"I thought so," I said. "I didn't know all the words, either."

"Yeah, but I have an excuse," Bob assured me. "I wasn't around when everybody was singing that song."

"Why? Where were you?"

"Vietnam."

*   *   *

Saturday when I went to the Chateau, the woman on duty told me Adele was at the sing-along and she left word for me to meet her there. The woman told me that to get to the sing-along all I had to do was take the elevator up to the second floor and walk straight down the corridor until I heard the singing. I had never gone upstairs before, and I was a little nervous about what I might find.

I remembered the third floor of the first nursing home my grandmother lived in for a few weeks before she was moved over to the Darrow Plaza. I could see myself stepping off the elevator with my mother. Nobody was in sight, but you could hear old people whimpering and screaming from every doorway.

"I'm not crazy, am I?" my grandmother wailed when we walked into her room. They had lifted the sides on her bed so she looked like she was in a crib. "What am I doing in here?"

"Promise me if I ever get old and sick like that you'll just go out in the yard with me and shoot me," my mother sobbed in the parking lot.

"I promise," I said. But when the time came, she died inside the house.

"Are you sure it's okay for me to go up there?" I asked the Chateau administrator.

"Of course." She smiled. "Everybody is invited to the sing-along."

When I got off the elevator, the second floor was dead. I tried not to look inside any of the open rooms. I heard singing and I picked up speed. Music was a sign that life was ahead. At the end of the hallway I turned and walked into a cluster of old people in wheelchairs with a radio among them. The people looked like they must have had Alzheimer's, and the radio was playing the Alicia Bridges hit:

I love the nightlife
I've got to boogie
On the disco round.

"Is this the sing-along?" I asked. A nurse came and pointed two doors down to the Activities Room. This was much better.

The Activities Room was full up with people. The group was starting to sing "Over There," and the nurse kept pointing for me to sit in the only available chair in the room, the one next to Adele. Adele was saving the chair for me, and it was obvious nobody else wanted it anyway, since Adele was singing like her life depended on it.

Over there
Over there
Over there, say a prayer
Over there . . .

"Remember that song from World War I?" Adele asked, like we had been there together.

Johnny, the Hawaiian-chicken-hula-man, walked through the aisles handing out the songbooks. I had never seen him smile before.

"You're going to love these, honey," he said, putting the book into my hands. "These were the *real* rock and roll."

An old woman with pigtails and dressed like Little Bo Peep was leading the group with all her might. Some mouths moved, but mostly everyone looked comatose. I figured they just had to warm up.

"Let's open our songbooks to page two," Bo Peep said. "Tea for

Two." She pushed the button on a boom box, and a piano began playing the introduction. I couldn't take my eyes off a woman shuffling back and forth across the room with her head bobbing up and down. She had on a Ralph Lauren sweater and pants that smelled like urine, and all she kept repeating was "Why, oh why, oh why" like a chant. She wouldn't stop until she was standing in front of someone's chair, perched to sit down on her lap.

"Oh, I loved this one." Adele piped up loud on the next song.

> *Ma, he's making eyes at me!*
> *Ma, he's awful nice to me.*
> *Ma, he's almost breaking my heart.*
> *Mercy, I'm beside him.*
> *Let his conscience guide him.*
> *Ma, he wants to marry me*
> *And be my honey bee.*
> *Every minute he gets bolder,*
> *Now he's leaning on my shoulder.*
> *Ma, he's kissing me.*

Adele was incredible. She remembered every word without being able to read them on the page. She was singing out as if this was seventy years ago when she was young, and everything she was singing for still sounded to her like the truth.

The woman in front of us kept turning to see who was sitting behind her. "I'm getting hoarse just listening to her," the woman complained to me. "What page are we supposed to be on?"

"Five Foot Two!" Bo Peep called out. "Does anyone remember 'Five Foot Two'?"

Yes, I did. But I couldn't remember why. Maybe my mother sang that around the house when I was little or I saw it once on my grandma's TV set. But here I was forty years later, and I knew every word to every song.

> *We ain't got a barrel of money*
> *Maybe we're ragged and funny.*
> *But we're walking along,*
> *Singing a song*
> *Side by side.*

"Oh, I wish they would do this here every day." Adele squeezed my hand.

> *Over there*
> *Over there*
> *Over there, say a prayer.*
> *Over there.*

"Oh, crud." Adele stomped her foot. "This is why I don't like coming to the Alzheimer's sing-along. They just sing the same song over and over again. Does anyone know 'Let Me Call You Sweetheart'?" Adele called out.

I cringed. Adele didn't have to see the dirty looks I was getting that were meant for her. Bo Peep stopped the tape.

"Good idea, Adele," she said, thumbing through the songbook. "Page eleven, everybody. Turn to page eleven!"

> *Let me call you sweetheart*
> *I'm in love with you.*
> *Let me hear you whisper*
> *That you love me, true.*

Adele put her hand on her heart and smiled up at the ceiling. I looked around and in at least some slight way everyone's mouth was moving. I was singing along with the group like I hadn't sung since I was in day camp.

Keep your love light shining
With your eyes so blue.
Let me call you sweetheart,
I'm in love with you.

"I'm so glad you're here." Adele held my hand. "I would have felt terrible if you missed this."

"Me, too," I said. And I meant it.

"These are the songs that never die," Adele said with pride.

"What page are we on again?" the woman in front of us turned around to ask me.

I looked down at page eleven. I suddenly had a memory of my eleventh birthday when I was president of my Beatles fan club and my father gave me my first Beatles songbook. I could see the words as if John and Paul were still singing them to me off the page.

One day thirty-five years from now, I could be living in a place like this, sitting at the sing-along and singing "She Loves You." I would still remember to shake my head at just at the right places as Paul once did. Across the room, a sweet middle-aged thing would be sitting beside her mother. I would watch her. She would know every word of the song as if she had been born in the 1950s, but she wouldn't really know how or why. I would smile knowingly. It was because my generation could not be forgotten. It was because whatever was coming down the road for us, everything was going to be all right.

Yeah, yeah, yeah, YEAH!

Why Am I Still Here?

Two weeks later I was feeling especially old. I knew this was in part because I had just finished writing a chapter book for kids. It was the last book in a series I had under contract, and I had been dragging myself and my editor through the rewrite for weeks.

Now when I slam-dunked my envelope into the Federal Express box for New York, I felt not unlike how I imagined a mother felt when she sent her last child off to college—lost. I didn't know what I was supposed to do with myself. I just knew I didn't have another word left in me.

I felt frightened that in middle age, after wanting to write for kids since I was sixteen, I had turned into my least favorite kind of children's book character—the confused little bear who didn't know what she was. But whatever she was, she knew she didn't want to be that.

For months I had been struggling in the back of my mind with what other jobs I could do when I finished this book because I was certain it would be time to move on from writing. I was thinking I could sell real estate or get a job in a public relations office or be an astronaut. Now it was starting to look like what I was to do next was apply for a job at the Chateau. That way I could see Adele three times a day. I could get a job in the dining room and learn to be one of the hair-net people.

For right now I didn't even want to go there.

All week I didn't go see Adele, and I didn't call or send a postcard like it said to do in the Adoption Manual. I decided I would wait until Saturday to see her again. I would see her once a week like I committed to in the first place. I didn't need to spoil this woman rotten by giving her all of my time.

I didn't sleep well at all that week. It was in the middle of one night when the answer came to me. It was in my chapter books. I had written them all about a feisty, adventurous girl named Annie Bananie, an eight-year-old who led her little friends in and out of trouble. But at the end of each story, the one character who really saves the day is an old woman named Grandma Gert.

Grandma Gert was based on my grandmother as I remember her when I was little and she lived in the flat above ours in Chicago. The fictitious Grandma Gert was tough and funny and sometimes deaf and wise. But the one thing she was, consistently, was old. She was old and she was the real heroine, and I had been writing about her for two years before I even knew Adele existed. It dawned on me that even before these books, I had written a picture book about somebody's fictitious old great-aunt and before that a book about an old shoe-shine lady. I had been writing kids' books about old women stars for years, perhaps unconsciously hoping to teach kids to like old people in case the day ever came that I became one. I sat up in bed stunned. My psyche had been prepping me for this day for years, and I didn't even know it.

Before that moment it hadn't occurred to me I would write a word about Adele and certainly not for kids. I knew adults were more frightened of old people than children. I had never written a book for grown-ups before. I got incredibly excited, but then within minutes I reconsidered. The whole thing was too much of a long shot. I decided I would talk it over with Adele, if for no other reason than that it would give us something interesting to discuss on Saturday morning if all there was to do in the Chit Chat Room was stare at really bad wallpaper.

Saturday morning, when I got to the Chateau, Adele was sitting next to Mary on the sofa. They looked like two old friends who had been sitting together for hours and decided to take a little snooze. Adele opened her eyes.

"Leah?" She reached for my hand. "Did you drive your jalopy here?"

"Of course." I laughed. "Why? Did you want to go out cruising?"

"That's the ticket!" Adele quickly lifted herself from the sofa. "Let's get out of this dump!"

I told Adele to wait right there. I wasn't going to have time to explain to her that mentally well people in L.A. did not get in the car just to go for a drive. Adele was ready to take me for an adventure. I went to pull my car up to the doorway. I couldn't get over a hideous image that kept recurring in my mind: me breaking down in the middle lane of the freeway in the ninety-degree heat with a ninety-three-year-old woman by my side. I visualized the inside of my trunk where there were no flares, bottles of water, or spare gym shoes in case we had to do some serious walking. I had never been in a car and responsible for a blind person before, but I figured if the Chateau was going to let me walk right out the front door with Adele as if I were her family, I could have faith that everything was going to be all right.

"Are you sure you don't want to come with us?" Adele asked Mary.

"Oh, no, honey." Mary walked us outside like she was seeing off the *Titanic.* "You two go ahead."

I opened the car door for Adele and helped her inside. The seatbelt alarm sounded, and Adele put her talking watch up to her ear.

"I must have set my alarm by mistake," she said. "What time is it?"

"It's eleven o'clock," I told her. "But that's not your watch. Those bells are just to remind you to put your seat belt on. May I help you?" I asked, strapping her in. "I'm not trying to get fresh."

"I didn't think you were that kind of girl," Adele said. "I missed you. It's good to talk to you. Mary and I have absolutely nothing to talk about. Absolutely nothing goes on in there. I even said to Mary, 'We have nothing to talk about.'"

"What did she say?" I asked.

"Nothing!"

I suggested to Adele maybe she could start up a conversation with somebody else. "There's got to be at least one interesting person."

"There aren't many in their right mind," Adele said. "They're all in various stages of falling apart in there."

"I'm sure you're right," I said, turning onto the ramp of the San Diego Freeway. "But if it's any consolation, they're all in various stages of falling apart out here, too. The only difference is out here they have driver's licenses."

"Get out." Adele got annoyed. "I don't need bolstering."

"I know that," I said, as if I did. "And I'm not trying to bolster you." I was trying to forget the only person Adele really did have in there was me.

"Some days I wonder why I'm still alive. What purpose could God possibly still have in mind for me?" Adele asked, like I was supposed to know the answer. "What am I still doing here?"

What are you doing here? You're being chauffeured out of the broiler Valley and down to the ocean. You're getting everything you asked for! "Well, one thing I know you're doing here for sure is changing my life," I said. "I think about you all the time. And I was thinking maybe I could write a new book."

"What's the subject matter?" Adele asked.

"I want to write about you and me and our friendship."

Adele perked up. "Get out!" she said. "You can't be serious."

"I think I may be serious."

"Oh, my God in heaven." Adele laughed with delight. "In my lifetime I never dreamed something like this would happen. Maybe I should just start from the beginning of my life and tell you everything. Did I ever tell you about our first car? It was a Graham Page. It was one of the very good ones. I don't know what you'd call them today."

"Maybe like a luxury sedan. A Mercedes. Did you ever drive?"

"I started when the kids were very little," Adele said, like I was taking dictation. "But my eyes weren't so keen then already, and I never did get a license. My husband used to take me out for drives like this." Adele smiled. "We used to drive all the way to the cemetery where our headstones would be."

"That sounds like a pleasant destination."

"And how." Adele laughed.

"But today we're heading to the beach," I told her, like she would be thrilled at the prize I was giving her.

"Did I ever tell you my mother sold stocks for the Klaxon Horn?

Remember the Klaxon Horn? It was the first car horn that was ever made." Adele spelled it out for me. "K-L-A-X-O-N."

I asked Adele to refresh my memory. "It sat outside of the car, but you diddled it from the inside," Adele said.

"Oh, my God, right! They were the horns you squeezed that went *aooga, aooga.* Right?"

"Something like that." Adele laughed. *"Aooga, aooga."*

In my lifetime I never could have dreamed I would be going for a drive with someone who once had a Klaxon Horn. I was enchanted. Adele threw her head back and the sun shined through her hair. We were two girlfriends laughing on our way to the beach. I turned on the radio.

"Did I ever tell you we were one of the first families on our block to have a radio?" Adele asked. "It was the Atwater Kent," she said, like she was reading the name in front of her. "I remember we would put it on the table and people would open their windows to hear music coming out of the box. Sometimes we would listen to Radio Free Europe or Ma Perkins. Do you know Ma Perkins?"

"I think I've heard of her."

"These things may not all connect now," Adele said, "but later you can pull them and string them together for the book."

Then Adele turned, and I could tell she was looking at me like she suddenly realized I was crazy. "Who is going to buy a thing like this?" she said.

"Maybe no one," I assured her. "It isn't a book yet. It may never be. So far it's just an idea. I don't even know that I can write it."

"What do you mean?" Adele questioned too loudly. "Of course you can. And I think it's a great idea."

"You do?"

"Absolutely," Adele said with the fervor of a Super Bowl coach. "You can do it. You have the talent for it. You'll just do it section by section. Not that you need me to tell you how to write a book. You have my blessing. If you want, I can even help you."

I felt faintly nauseous. I didn't know how to say I was moved by how inherently Adele seemed to understand the process. But I was hoping that I hadn't gotten myself in deeper than I had imagined. "I sort of have to write by myself," I said.

"I figured that's how most writers do it," Adele said without missing a beat. "I understand. But if you need them, I can give you some tips from time to time. Not that you need me to help you write."

A writer always needs help to write.

Adele hit the button on her talking watch. It was 11:30. We were still ten minutes from the ocean, and Adele was afraid we wouldn't get to the Chateau in time for the lunch lineup. I turned around and headed back.

"I can tell we're back on the freeway," Adele said. "It's noisy."

She held her hand up in front of her like she was off in her own world. I recalled for the first time ever being in my father's '58 Oldsmobile as he drove down Lake Shore Drive. I would sit beside him and hold up my thumb to the sun because it was shining in my face. I was amazed at how my thumb could always cover the entire sun. I never told my father I could do that, because I didn't think he would understand that a little girl could have so much power.

"I can see brighter where the sun is," Adele said.

I asked Adele if she could see her hand.

"No," Adele said.

"But you know it's there."

"Yes. I know it's there."

"I think you just described faith," I said. "You can't see it but you know it's there."

"Absolutely." Adele felt for my hand. "Absolutely. It's there. It's like your book. You just can't see it yet. But believe me. I know. Book is my middle name."

I envied her confidence.

"I'll tell you anything you want to know. After all," Adele said, "I didn't commit any crimes or anything."

"Well, hurry up and do something." I tried to laugh. "It's a jungle out there. I'm probably going to need some good dirt if anybody is going to want to buy this book."

"Now that's using your noodle!" Adele laughed.

Up ahead was the spot where the San Diego Freeway intersected with the 101. I couldn't see it yet, but I knew it was there and that traffic would jam up there and go bumper to bumper because it always did. When that happened, I would have to alleviate Adele's fears that we'd be stuck sitting when the lunch lineup was already forming.

Adele lifted her face to the sun. We were in the middle lane doing sixty with the a/c humming. We cruised straight through. With Adele by my side, everything was going to be all right.

WALKING WITH A PURSE FULL OF TREASURES

The next week Bob broke up with his girlfriend, and he left L.A. for a few days to chill out. Suddenly I noticed walking got very lonely. I happened to mention that to Jenny when she called from her car phone.

"Who is this Bob guy? If you've been walking with him for two years, how come I'm just hearing about him for the first time?"

"Because he's just somebody I walk with," I told Jenny. "I never thought about him to talk about him. He's a wonderful, decent guy for the park, but that's it. There's nothing more there. He's blue-collar. He doesn't make much money. He goes to bed at nine o'clock. Get the picture?"

"I think so," Jenny said. "But what's the problem?"

The problem was I missed my walking buddy. So I went to the Chateau to fetch Adele. Joanna, at the front desk, told me Adele was out on the patio. The patio was where people went if they wanted to smoke or just get some fresh air. I spotted Adele and Mary alone together off in the corner. Their eyes were closed. Adele was holding her pocketbook close to her chest like she always did. I realized today for the first time that Adele was the only woman there who always carried a purse. She was ninety-three and still a lady.

"Hi, Adele. Want to leave this joint and take a walk with me?"

"And how." Adele lifted herself quickly from the chair. I asked Mary if she wanted to join us, but she said she wanted to stay right there and read, although there wasn't a printed page in sight.

Adele took my arm, and we started slowly for the front door. I didn't expect this to be like a walk around the track, but I thought Adele might get a better workout without her pocketbook on her arm and I asked if she wanted to drop it off in her room.

"Oh, no," Adele said without hesitation. "I don't let this out of my sight."

We headed outside and Adele put her purse strap over her shoulder, like a street-savvy little girl who got her first purse and was transporting her treasures in it. I couldn't help thinking that the most valuable thing she was carrying around in there was her pride. What could she have been guarding?

"Oh, it's beautiful out here," Adele said. "This is nice walking like this with you." It was. But even for almost ninety-four she was walking too slowly.

"Can we pick up the pace just a little bit? It will put hair on your chest."

"Now that's what I'm looking for," Adele said. Then she started to sing:

> *The old gray mare, she ain't what she used to be,*
> *Ain't what she used to be, ain't what she used to be.*

"Are you saying we're going too fast?"

"My legs hurt today for some reason," Adele said. "I never had pain in my legs before."

Was she kidding? I got pains from time to time. She was fifty years older than me. I had been getting pains in my legs and feet since I was thirty-seven.

"Well, I don't. My feet are perfect," Adele bragged. "No corns or bunions. Plus, I have a Yankee foot."

"What's a Yankee foot?" I almost didn't want to know.

"Long and narrow," Adele said, as if my feet weren't normal. "That's why I don't understand why at my age I have this pain."

I looked at Adele's purse. I had never held it before or looked at it in this way. "Is it possible you're in pain from carrying your pocketbook? It looks like it might be kind of heavy."

"I can't imagine what I would have in here that would make this so heavy." Adele was surprised. Then she handed it to me. "Can you?"

"What have you got in here? A bowling ball?"

"Is it so heavy?" Adele wanted to know. "How could it be that heavy? I don't know what I've got in there besides my cane. Maybe you should go through my purse. But not right here, do you think? I don't want to give anybody ideas."

The street was heavy with traffic and an occasional hooker. I figured nobody would be so low as to try to rob an old blind lady. I walked Adele over to the bench by the tree where we liked to sit. Nobody could really see us there, and the only thing in sight was a garbage can. Adele opened her pocketbook for me to take a peek. A stack of folded Kleenex was on top. Climbing up the side of the stack were three ants.

"Is it a law that after you reach a certain age you have to carry around a ream of Kleenex?" I asked her.

"It's clean." Adele defended the supply.

"That's true," I tried to say extra gently. "Did you know you have ants in it?"

"Ants? What are you talking about?"

"I think it's because of all these crumbs I'm feeling on the bottom," I said. "Good God, there're a lot of crumbs down there. Are you putting food in your pocketbook in the dining room?"

"Of course not," Adele insisted. "Not in the dining room. Only when I go to the Seniors' Center. I bring my brownie back for my roommate. She likes that. Or sometimes I bring some leftover brisket from lunch if I have any. Are you sure those are ants? We've got to get them out. I've never had ants in my life!"

"You have ants in your pants." I laughed.

"Quiet, you." Adele tried not to giggle. "Just be careful inside there. What else have I got?"

"What's this?" I asked, lifting a handful of sugar. "Cocaine? Oh— I see. It's packs of sugar. It's ripped. You've got a thousand packs of sugar in here. You need to keep these for any reason?"

"It's perfectly good sugar!"

"I'm sure the ants would agree."

"Okay, so throw it out," Adele conceded. "Just don't throw out my loot while you're at it." Adele reached into her purse and handed me a thin little billfold. It looked like it was handmade. "How much do I have in there?"

There was a twenty-dollar bill folded with a paper clip on it. "My husband made the wallet for me," Adele said. "I've had it forty years." Then Adele slowly lifted out a makeup bag. It was stuffed with costume jewelry. There were handfuls of screw-on earrings that didn't look like they all had matches, a frog brooch, and some pins. It did not all look like old-lady jewelry. Some of it was quite beautiful, deserving special little boxes.

"I hope it's all here," Adele said, trying to hold each piece in her fingers.

"There's certainly lots of it," I said. "It looks heavy. That could be what's making your purse so heavy. Do you like to carry the jewelry bag with you?"

"I don't like to," Adele said. "But I have to. I can't leave it in my room or they'll take it."

"Who will take it?" I asked. "They steal things right out of your room?"

"Sure," Adele said, like she was accepting the ways of the world. "Last year someone broke in and stole my long underwear."

"Someone wanted your underwear?"

"Of course," Adele said. "It was perfectly good underwear. The expensive kind. They took it right from my dresser. I may have even been in the room when it happened."

I wanted to cry because I knew Adele wasn't just having a bout of dementia and she was telling me the truth. How desperately bored and angry did a person have to be to steal a blind woman's long underwear?

"Is the stone on this purple?" Adele asked, reaching for a necklace from her bag. It was a pretty amethyst. "Then this is my most special necklace. What does it look like?"

I looked around to make sure nobody else was looking. "It's attractive. Very classy looking."

"Well, yes, it should be. It was expensive." Adele held it up to her heart. " My children bought it for me. This is my *fermegan*. Do you know the word? It's Yiddish. It means treasure."

"No wonder you keep it by your side," I said. It was making sense now. I felt happy to see Adele with a connection to her children. Also, strangely, in that moment, I felt like I had lost her to faces I would never meet.

"I think when they bought it they said it cost about a hundred dollars," Adele said too loudly. "And that was already a few years ago, right after my pearls were stolen here. The pearls were from my husband. Of course I kept looking and hoping someone would bring them back, but it was no use. I'll never get them back. They were the only piece of jewelry I had left from him. So then my children sent me this necklace."

I couldn't believe it. This woman had to carry what was left of her prized possessions around with her like a homeless person. Now all she had left to hold on to of any meaning was the gift from her children, not knowing when that might be taken from her as well.

"This is horrible!" I said, closing the pocketbook. "Isn't there somewhere they can lock this stuff up for you? You have a beautiful necklace. I mean, this is all you've got! It's your *fermegan*."

I started back to the Chateau, and Adele held my arm tight. "You're my *fermegan*," Adele said softly. "You're all I've got."

All Dolled Up at the Beauty Parlor

The next week I needed a haircut. I was walking around the track alone, annoyed that Bob had not come back yet. I realized I had gotten used to seeing him right after I walked out of the salon, when my hair looked perfect. Bob and I gave each other really good haircut critiques. Now I was thinking if I was waiting for Bob, something was terribly off. I needed something different.

I made an appointment with somebody new who I heard was hip and sensational, and I came out of there with the haircut from hell. What made this haircut particularly bloodcurdling was that I had had the exact same haircut from the exact same stylist only at a different salon when I was in my thirties. But I couldn't remember any of that until it was already too late and I was in shock and on my way out the door looking like a middle-aged bull terrier. The good news was this time, being older, I at least had enough self-esteem to walk out of there without leaving a tip.

I got into my car, looked at myself in the mirror, and burst into tears. I didn't know how I was going to drive, but I knew I had to go somewhere where I wouldn't be seen.

"Tell me what's bothering you," Adele said when I got to her door. I sat in the rocker, and Adele held my hand the way my mother used to do when I was upset as a little girl.

"I got a haircut," I said.

Then I waited. I needed someone to comfort me.

"I could use a haircut," Adele said. "It's a little long, don't you think?"

"What?"

"There's a beauty shop room in the Chateau where I ordinarily go for my cuts," Adele went on, "but I've heard of a real beauty parlor I would try if only I had someone to take me there and help show them what I want."

I volunteered. Already I started to feel a little better. This would be another new experience Adele and I could share. What concerned me, though, was that I was still angry and hair deranged enough that I didn't want Adele's salon experience to be any better than mine.

The next morning Adele and I headed down the street to Maria's Hair Salon. Maria herself was waiting for Adele at the door. She was glad to see Adele back even though Adele had no recollection of being there once before.

"Oh, sure." Maria winked. "You mean you've forgotten me already? Someone brought you here from the Chateau about six months ago."

"Well, I'm sure you're probably right," Adele said. "I just don't remember. Were you the one who cut my hair last time?"

"That's right," Maria said. "And I'll cut it again today. You want a wash, cut, and set. Right?"

"Of course!" Adele said too loudly. "The works!"

"The works!" Maria laughed. Then she took Adele's arm and led her off.

"I just want it cut to the nape of the neck." Adele pointed. "That sounds good. Isn't that right, Leah?"

Maria looked at my hair like I needed a conservator to make those decisions.

"Don't worry, Adele," Maria said in a thick accent. "I'll cut it just where you want it."

"I used to have a thick head." Adele relaxed her head into the washbowl. "I mean of hair." She took off her glasses. With her head tilted back I could see her features differently. I could tell how pretty she must have been when she was young. She smiled like she was enjoying every second of the warm water and shampoo without the slightest anticipation of what was coming next.

"Wait until you're my age," Adele said. "I'm going to be ninety-four in a few weeks. You won't care about what your hair looks like. You just want it to be neat."

For the first time I heard something about old age that sounded worth living for. I had never heard Adele sound so casual and wise. She smiled to herself. She looked strong and present in that chair. Nothing could harm her. Maria wrapped a towel around Adele's head, like a maharanil on her way to the hair-cutting station. I followed at her feet.

"In the twenties everybody wore side combs," Adele said. "There weren't beauty parlors for women yet back then. We had to go to the barber shop. Yup," Adele said slowly. "Those were the days. Can you imagine?"

"It's hard to imagine." Maria was totally intrigued.

Maybe so, but could Adele imagine going through what I had just been through? Could she picture a salon where men wore midriff tops and the women stood all day in shoes with platforms like the ones you used to wear if you had polio? Could Adele dig a disco rap pounding in her hearing aid while a team of green-haired nymphettes with rings in their belly buttons wrapped her head in enough tinfoil for her to pick up the news reports on Radio Free Europe? Could Adele trust a place where everybody's name was Paolo or Georges, and they shamed you into leaving more money for the tips than Maria charged for "the works"? Did Adele think being beautiful today was so easy?

Adele gazed straight into the mirror while Maria cut. Adele looked good and she knew it. Maria took Adele's arm and walked her over to the dryers with a hundred curlers in her hair.

"Leah?" Adele called out. "What are you going to do while you're waiting?" I said I was going to work on the book proposal. "What's the subject matter?" Adele asked.

"It's about our friendship. Remember?"

"Read it to me," Adele said. "I'll tell you if it's any good!" Then Maria lowered the spaceship down over Adele's head.

"Believe it or not, my hair was thick and curly like yours until I turned ninety," Adele said loudly, feeling for my hand.

It was just a matter of time. In a few weeks my hair could still grow back. I would go back to my regular stylist to be cut and gelled and weaved and dyed, but when all was said and done, no matter how much I did to make my hair look good, this is where I'd end up: drying up under the spaceship.

The bell went off, and Maria took out the curlers and brushed and teased Adele's hair into a perfect old-lady bubble. Adele turned her head from side to side like she was checking herself out in the mirror.

"You're all dolled up and ready for your date tonight, Adele." Maria winked.

"And how." Adele laughed as she waved good-bye. "I already had my one special date."

Everyone in the salon was smiling. Adele didn't know how adorable she was. She was leaving in total peace with her haircut.

Outside it was warm and there was a slight breeze. Adele was a little wobbly on her feet. She broke into song, tipsy from sitting under the dryer so long.

> *Enjoy yourself, while you are in the pink.*
> *Enjoy yourself, it's later than you think.*
> *Time goes by, faster than a wink.*
> *So enjoy yourself, while you're still in the pink.*

"Remember that song? I think it was from my mother's day. What color is my hair? Is there still any brown left or is it all gray?"

"There's a little brown," I said. "Maria did a really good job. You look very pretty."

"Do you think it will stay until tomorrow?" Adele sounded more serious. "How do I sleep on it? With a hairnet?"

"Sure," I said. "It will probably look good again when you wake up."

"What difference does it make if I look good?" Adele suddenly got very quiet. "I still don't have any friends."

"I'm your friend," I said. "And I think you're beautiful." I held Adele's hand the way my mother used to hold mine when there was nothing she could do to save me from the ways of the world.

"You never know," I said. "You could meet someone special tomorrow."

"Horse feathers." Adele started to walk. The wind came up. Adele held her hair in place.

Vanity was the hope eternal.

George Clooney, Scabies, and Incarceration of the Elderly

A few days later, for a change of pace from being with and writing about Adele, I went to the Warner Brothers lot to meet my friend Kathy for lunch. When I pulled up to the gate, I couldn't believe what a rush it was to be in the "real world" again, even if this was just television. I figured two hours of the young and the dramatic before I went back to the Chateau would be plenty—just what the doctor ordered.

"I haven't seen you for months." Kathy hugged me at her trailer. "What have you been up to? Catch me up on all the dirt."

Kathy was in a new hit series. We walked by the *Friends* set and the studio where they filmed *ER,* past the commissary, and straight to Kathy's table in the VIP restaurant. I tried to entertain her with all the dirt I knew, which was that Adele's friend Mary had been quarantined for days and Adele was afraid that Mary had a terminal disease since the doctor at the Chateau wouldn't tell her squat. I was telling her that Adele wanted me to ask another doctor about the illness, and then all of a sudden, George Clooney walked in. He was heading right toward our table.

He had on a stethoscope over his T-shirt, along with shorts and tennis shoes without socks. He was tan and healthy and the sexiest doctor alive, with a smile that could melt a tumor.

"Hi, Kathy." He extended his hand. "George Clooney. I really like your work."

Kathy told him she liked his work, too. They congratulated each other on their shows, and then Anthony Edwards, Noah Wylie, and some others from the medical staff of *ER* walked in and sat with Clooney at the very next table. They were reading script pages and eating hamburgers and laughing. Then in no time everybody had to get back for rehearsals, and Kathy, Clooney, and I ended up walking out of the restaurant together. George smiled and waved good-bye as he drove away down the lot on his personalized studio golf cart.

Twenty minutes later I was holding open the door for an old, bald guy backing his electric wheelchair into the Chateau lobby. But I couldn't find Adele. I looked all over the building until finally I spotted her in the Activities Room. They were having the Friday afternoon religious service. Every other week they alternated religious preferences. Today Adele was mumbling and praying for something I couldn't understand. In front of the room the world's homeliest rabbi was blessing what looked to be a bottle of Thunderbird.

"What's new?" Adele asked me. "I'm here praying for Mary. She's still quarantined. Today I found out why. It's scurvy."

"Scurvy?" I tried not to sound frightened.

"Yes," Adele said. "Can a person die from that?"

"I don't think so," I said although I couldn't remember what scurvy even was.

"They say it's what I have," Adele tried to whisper. "Dr. Campbell said I have the scurvy marks all over my arm. Just like Mary. But I don't see any marks."

I looked at Adele's arm. It was covered with red bumps.

"I'm not sure if I'm even supposed to be here," Adele said, scratching herself. "They may have said I had to wait in my room, but I don't remember. I think they said you can get it from just touching somebody. But I never touch anybody. Mary has to stay in her room for a month. Oh, God, if they incarcerate me for a month, I'll die in there."

"The time is now to turn the spotlight not on others, but on ourselves," Rabbi Rothstein began his sermon. "We are not God's puppets. But God gave us freedom, freedom of choice. Our job is to choose what's right."

My heart was pounding. I tried to move my hand, but Adele was holding it tight.

"I just have to go to the bathroom," I told her.

"You'll be back?" Adele asked.

"I'll be right back. I promise."

I got up and walked down the hall to the front desk. Then I did something that only a child of Satan would do. I ratted on Adele.

"She knows she's not supposed to be out of her room," Joanna, the administrator, said. "Dr. Campbell was here and he told her. Adele has scabies."

"Scabies? Not scurvy?"

"No, scabies. Little scabs on the skin. It's highly contagious. They won't kill you, but they itch like hell and they can spread like wildfire in a place like this where there's old people. That's all I need in here, an epidemic," the administrator said, heading for the Activities Room. "It's bad enough Mary and Adele have it. So thanks for the tip. We really appreciate it."

"It's not a problem," I said. Then I turned and walked right out the door. I drove home and spent the rest of the afternoon showering and trying to fight off the image in my mind of Adele in the Activities

Room praying with all her heart, only to be lifted up from her seat and locked away in L-7. She would never have reason to have faith again, least of all in me. I did what I had to do when I told on Adele, but now I had to do whatever it took to get her out of that place.

I woke up the next morning scratching. I couldn't tell if I was just imagining the red spots on my arm, but I called the Chateau before I went over there anyway.

"It's not exactly a hundred percent that you would catch it," the girl on the phone said. "But it's pretty possible. Just as long as Adele didn't touch you, you should be fine. But I wouldn't come see her today if I were you. Don't worry. Adele may be out of quarantine by tomorrow."

"Wonderful! Will you give her this message? Tell her I love her and I'll wait for her and see her tomorrow."

"Sure," the girl said. "No problem."

Three days later I was scratching and talking to Adele through her door since they wouldn't let me go inside.

"Did they give you my message that I love you?"

"I didn't get any messages. I'm in hell. But you—you're heaven-sent."

"No, I'm not." I cringed. "You don't know."

"If you step outside yourself and look in, you can see why," Adele said. "You really are like an angel. I mean it. Do you believe me?"

"Yes," I said, ready to cry. "Do you believe me?"

"Of course!" Adele said with all her heart. "I just wish I could see you."

"Don't worry. They told me at the front desk all they have to do is give you a scabies treatment, then Dr. Campbell comes back here to check that the scabies are gone and you're free. It will only be another two days."

At the end of the first week, Adele had her scabies treatment, but then Dr. Campbell left town for his vacation in Palm Beach. They told me at the front desk he would be back in five days. Adele was just expected to sit in there. I guess they figured that was all she did anyway.

"They only sent me one book from Braille this week," Adele complained to me through the door. "It's called *Hitler's Willing Executioner.* Do I need that in here?"

"Probably not," I said. I told Adele I'd call Braille to have them send over better books on tape. "Your roommate isn't in there with you, is she?"

"No," Adele said. "They had to take her back to the hospital again in the middle of the night. Of course Lorraine didn't have scurvy, so she wasn't incarcerated in here, anyway."

"Do you think Lorraine would mind if you turned on her television?" I asked. "Can you find the television? Then you would at least have some human company to listen to for just a few more days."

"I have my talking watch to tell me what time it is," Adele said. "Besides, I wouldn't want to diddle around to find the television and there's nothing on, anyway. It doesn't matter. I don't think I'm even going to make it a few more days."

"Of course you'll make it." I tried to cheer her on. I just didn't know how I would. I was constantly nervous about Adele in there, and it frightened me that without her I had little to look forward to but my daily constitutional in the park with Bob, who had just gotten back into town.

"What if in the last six weeks I accidentally touched you while we were walking?" I asked Bob at the park that night. "The incubation period is six weeks."

"Are you kidding?" Bob teased me. "You've 'accidentally' not been able to keep your hands off me for the last three years."

"Right." I could feel myself blushing. "Then it's settled. You've got scabies."

"I've had worse," Bob boasted. He pretended to get real macho. "Remember who you're talking to—Mr. Vietnam combat vet."

I looked at Bob. He was ridiculous, but he was my answer. I couldn't wait any longer for them to tell me Adele was better. I had to have the courage and conviction to napalm Adele's door.

I called my doctor to get my own prescription for the anti-scabies treatment. Then I smeared it on from head to toe. Forty-eight hours later I was ready to head down the Chateau hallway. Nobody was about to stop me. I got to Adele's room, prepared to charge my shoulder to the door, and discovered it was open. Adele was right there, dressed nicely like it was any other day. She was listening to her talking book, loud.

"Leah? Oh, thank God! I want to touch you but I can't."

"That's right," I told her. "You've got the cooties."

"Quiet, you! I've got scabies. Look!" Adele lifted her top so I could see her breast, and then she scratched herself. I had never seen a breast that long and old before. "I'm not wearing a bra!"

"Well, you're living dangerously." I tried to talk like she was just one of the girls. "You're not leaving the room."

Neither was Lorraine. She had just come back from the hospital the night before, and they quarantined her.

"She doesn't care," Adele insisted as if Lorraine wasn't in the room. "Lorraine stays in here all day anyway except when she goes to have her smokes."

"What do you mean she doesn't care?" I looked right at Lorraine. "She can't leave for meals or anything! Are you okay, Lorraine?"

"Mm hmm."

"Don't worry, Lorraine." Adele tried to be motivational. "We've lived through a lot worse in our lives, and we'll live through this, too. We must be strong. Leah will get us out of here."

It wasn't going to be that easy. Six days later, Dr. Campbell still had not come back from his vacation, and Adele's scabies had not gone away. When I got to Adele's that day, the TV was on. She was sitting in her rocker with her hair straight up, scratching her nipples and pretending to be watching *Montel Williams*. Empty food trays and the paper tins from a box of chocolates were all around the floor.

"I bet you two gals are really getting to know each other," I said.

"Mm hmm," Lorraine answered.

"We're going stir crazy in here." Adele hugged me. "Nobody tells us anything. If I so much as just stand in the doorway to get some air, they tell me to go back inside. I'm afraid they're going to keep me trapped in here until Christmas!"

"Don't worry, you'll be out of here long before Christmas," I told her. Then I went back to the front desk again to make sure I was right.

Fabian, the nighttime orderly, was on duty getting the Chateau ready for Halloween. He was hanging a spooky-looking banner over the door that said "Beware of Ghosts," which seemed like sound advice in a place like this at any time of year.

"Only three more days," Fabian told me. "I can't believe how fast Halloween crept up."

About as fast as Adele's scabies.

"I have to give Adele one more scabies treatment tomorrow," Fabian explained. "Doctor's orders." Hopefully this time all the scabs would disappear and Dr. Campbell would be coming to check Adele and say that she was free.

"How come you can't just tell Adele that?" I wanted to know. What would be so bad about treating these people with some dignity?

"Because we have to not tell them," Fabian said. "Otherwise if we say, for example, they'll get out earlier and then we find out it's longer, they get disappointed because they're so old."

"I'm getting so old being disappointed in here, too." I walked off. Adele was standing halfway out in the hall.

"What did they say? Why do I have to stay in here?" she pleaded.

"They said three more days. I know it's horrible," I told her, "but thank God you at least have Lorraine so you're not alone in here all day."

"Yes, but Lorraine gets out," Adele tattled. "She waits and then she sneaks out every night for a smoke. Maybe I'll sneak out tonight." Adele's face lit up with possibility.

"You might be a little more conspicuous. Besides, it could be dangerous."

"I'll walk up against the wall," Adele said. "Don't worry, I'll take my cane."

"Please wait for me." I held Adele's hand. "On Halloween, we'll get out of here together."

HALLOWEEN

Three days later I woke up determined to see to it that this was the day Adele was sprung from her prison, no matter what. I would probably have let the fact that it was also Halloween come and go, like I had every other Halloween since I was twelve, if Bob hadn't called that morning for the very first time to tell me Connie was going as a fireman. Connie was Bob's old dog. Bob was going as a cowboy, or if he could find any oatmeal in his house, he would smear it on his face and go as a cowboy/monster. "And you?" Bob laughed. "What are you going to be for Halloween?"

What was I going to be? Miserable. I was going to be a crusader for the old and scabied. Then I was going to work. I had a job to do. I was a writer on a deadline to finish my book proposal. I was going to be Jack Nicholson in his role in *The Shining,* only getting up from my typewriter long enough to hack someone with an ax or pelt children with M&M's. But it didn't occur to me that I could dress up, too. Suddenly it struck me that I was missing the point of life. I was embarrassed, and then I started to feel very light. I wasn't a kid, but fun was permitted. All I had to do was find it.

I scoured my closet for a costume. I found a gypsy scarf and an old black eye mask that I used for keeping out the sun, so I could either be Zorro or Kitty Carlisle on *What's My Line.* Twenty minutes later I was all dressed up with nowhere to go, and then I remembered to call the Chateau. They seemed to have a party there for every holiday, and they weren't going to let me down today. The Chateau Halloween bash was from one to two o'clock. Dr. Campbell was expected to be there no later than 12:30. This would work out perfectly. Adele would be released from quarantine in time for me to take her out to celebrate.

By 12:15 I had come to my senses and decided not to be the only person in costume at a party where most people hadn't ventured outside their bathrobes in a decade. I ditched my Kitty/Zorro garb, found an old pair of Groucho glasses, and tore out the door. When I got to the Chateau, they were setting up the party in the dining room and Adele was climbing the walls. Dr. Campbell had not been to her room yet, although one of the staff told her that he was in the building and that a Halloween party was about to start.

"And here you are, like an angel, coming to take me." Adele hugged me. "God knows I could use a good, peppy party." Adele almost wept. "I don't know why He put you in front of me."

"Because you wouldn't know I was there if I was behind you," I said, which was the closest I could get to saying God knew I would kill for "peppy." I told Adele I was going to find the doctor.

"Whatever you do, don't tell him about this," Adele said, scratching her nipple. "This one still itches. What if he finds out and he doesn't let me out of here? They'll let Lorraine go free, and I'll be in here by myself utterly alone. Oh, my God, for the first time in my life I think I'd have to pray to die."

"Don't worry," I said. "We're going to a party." Then I put my Groucho glasses on and headed for the front desk.

The girl on duty was dressed up as Minnie Mouse, and she was eating Kit Kat bars straight from a giant bag.

"I'm confused, Minnie," I said, "as I imagine ninety-nine percent of the people in this place are. But it's past twelve-thirty and Dr. Campbell still hasn't come to Adele's room. How many more people does he have to see before he gets to her?"

"Dr. Campbell?" Minnie answered. "None. This isn't Dr. Campbell's day to be here."

"What do you mean? They told me when I called this morning he would be here. Somebody on staff just told Adele they saw him here."

"They must have meant Dr. Rice," the girl said. "Dr. Rice was here but he left."

"Who is Dr. Rice?"

"Dr. Rice is the psychiatrist," Minnie said. "But Dr. Campbell doesn't come until tomorrow."

"Tomorrow?" I lost it. "Tomorrow's too late! Halloween is today!" I took my Groucho glasses off. Minnie Mouse looked at me like she was trying to figure out who I was supposed to be. Who was I? I was Shirley MacLaine in her famous hospital scene from *Terms of Endearment* where she stood at the nurse's station screaming for some idiot to bring Debra Winger her pain shot. Her daughter was not to be forgotten! Neither was Adele. Adele wasn't going to make it in that room any longer. And she was not going to miss that party. Did Minnie hear what I was saying? I had never spoken up so strongly for a person in my life. "Get Dr. Campbell on the phone now!"

At one o'clock sharp Dr. Campbell's office gave the word that Adele could be released from quarantine. Her roommate, Lorraine, could go to the party, too, but Lorraine was fast asleep. I tore down the hallway to get Adele. I knew we were late because no one else was in sight.

"Relax!" Minnie called after me, like she was afraid I was old enough to have a stroke. "Take your time. I mean this isn't your first Halloween, is it?"

No, but it might as well have been. As soon as we walked into the dining room I knew you haven't lived until you've seen a pirate in a wheelchair. He was right beside Uncle Sam and a man who was either supposed to be an old goat or a very old judge. The warthog was guarding the door dressed like a flapper from the roaring twenties. And then I saw something that took me by surprise. It was Adele's friend Mary. She had been released from six weeks of quarantine a few days earlier, and now she looked like she had come to the party as someone from *Night of the Living Dead*. Adele reached for Mary's hand, overjoyed.

"When you get older, you don't get better as fast," Mary said slowly.

"I'm too young to know about those things." Adele laughed. "I'm only going to be ninety-four next week. But I'm sure I got those scabies from you in the first place, Mary!" Adele said. "You can't get scabies twice, can you?"

I put my Groucho glasses on Adele and she had a good laugh, but what she really wanted to know was if anyone saw her scratching herself and what I did with the raffle ticket they gave us at the door in case the prize was some decent Halloween candy.

"If I win, I'll share it with you and Mary fifty-fifty," Adele said. "You be my eyes when they call the winner and tell me what I'm missing so I can try to visualize it. Okay?"

Certainly. Picture if you will, Adele, an afternoon on mescaline. There was a ghost with glasses next to a ghost in a fitted sheet beside a woman in a cap with a stuffed teddy bear who was either supposed to be an elf or a stray from a John Bradshaw workshop. One of the nurses took the hand of a man named Larry from the Alzheimer's section and walked him to the dance floor. I had seen Larry drop his pants more than once in the Chit Chat Room, and I was praying he wouldn't do it now or break into the lambada.

"Some of the people here are dressed in costumes," I told Adele.

"Really!" Adele was delighted. "I like this music!"

A hired musician played "La Cucaracha" on the saxophone like he was willing to bust his last artery for this gig, and everyone stared. A few people went out on the dance floor. The staff smiled at each other and at me knowingly. We were young and we knew something the old people couldn't know. Someday we would all know that the only reason Halloween had been for kids in the first place was because kids still had their teeth to eat the candy. But it was the seniors who were really made for trick or treating. They had lived long enough for their teeth to turn into genuine fangs and to walk like Frankenstein and be blind as a bat with scabies and the facial stare and mask of "the mummy." They had made it through a thousand "fright nights" and more "days of the dead" than they could remember. They had designed and earned their costumes and they knew it.

Some of the staff's children showed up as Dracula and Batman and Sheera, Goddess of Power, and everyone cooed over how undeniably adorable they were. But seeing them now reminded me of the night I watched a thirteen-year-old sing "I Did It My Way" at his bar mitzvah. They needed soul.

The Chateau administrator stopped the music to call out the winning raffle numbers. The winner was Don Ho, but Adele didn't care because the prize was Jergen's hand lotion and a six-pack of raisins.

"Being here was the prize." Adele squeezed my hand. "I'm so glad you came. I would have felt terrible if you missed all of this."

The sax man started to play "God Bless America," the equivalent of "last call," which meant the party was about to be over.

"I just hate for this to end," Adele said, singing her lungs out. "Now you're going to leave, and everything goes back to normal and everyone turns back into a bunch of corpses. Do you know what I mean?"

Did I ever. Adele and I started down the hallway. A cowboy came toward us on his walker with a toy holster and Sylvester and Tweetie Pie on his pockets. I had seen him many times before, but we had never said a word.

"Howdy, pardner," I said, tipping the Groucho glasses on Adele's head.

"Howdy yourself there, cowgirls." The man lifted the front of his walker like it was a horse standing on its hind legs.

God bless America. "Hi-yo, Silver, away!"

Turning Ninety-Four

On Adele's official ninety-fourth birthday, my friend Jenny called me from her car phone. She was on the Santa Monica freeway, driving illegally in the carpool lane so she had a chance in hell of getting to the airport in time to catch her flight to New York. I was excited and on my way out to the Chateau. I was going to celebrate the birthday event vicariously since I doubted I would ever have a ninety-fourth of my own.

"How is the old lady?" Jenny asked.

"It's her birthday," I said. "Can you imagine waking up one day and you look in the mirror and you're ninety-four years old?"

"Absolutely," Jenny said. "It happened this morning."

I left for the Chateau with a bouquet of flowers in a basket. I didn't know what else I was supposed to do to make Adele's birthday happy since I suspected the only thing that made a difference when you got that old was the thing that really mattered all along—being reminded of the people who love you because they write or call to tell you so. My wish for Adele's birthday was that somebody from her family would remember this day.

When I got to Adele's room, there was a big paper "Happy Birthday Bear" from the management with Adele's name written in on the bottom and signed "From Your Friends at the Chateau." I felt a little better already although I doubted Adele knew it was even there. Inside, Lorraine was asleep and Adele was sitting in her rocker opening and closing her jaw.

"This is the reason I don't look my age," Adele said, like she was giving me her ancient beauty secrets. "And I am at quite an age!"

"How old are you now?" I sang. "How old are you now?"

"I ain't tellin'. Ninety-four!" Adele boasted. "That's almost one hundred!"

"Almost!" I laughed.

"And don't forget you must have respect for age," Adele said sarcastically. "Because you only treat me as an equal."

"Oh, right, ma'am." I laughed. "I'll stop that right away." Then for a moment we just sat there. I never wanted to stop that. We were definitely equals. Neither one of us had ever expected to end up at the places in our lives where we were today. We were good friends, but I couldn't treat Adele exactly as one of my peers because she was younger at heart than most of them could be on their birthdays.

"How did you even know my birthday was today?" Adele tried to play coy.

"I saw it on the Internet."

"The what?"

"The Internet—it's on the computer. On the Internet you could tell the whole world at once 'Today is your day.' It's the biggest thing since the telephone."

"Oh, that sounds very interesting," Adele said. "I'd like to have one of those. Did I ever tell you we were one of the first families in Newark to have a telephone?"

"No. Really?"

"Back then if you wanted to dial somebody, you'd say, 'Hello, Central.'"

"Was that even before the days you cranked up the phone and said, 'Operator'?"

"Oh, sure," Adele said. "This was Alexander Graham Bell's phone, and they had that famous comedy routine about it. Have you ever heard it? 'Hello, Central. What number do you want?' 'What numbers do you got?'"

"Sure." Adele laughed. "Hello, Central" is as old as the hills and the hills behind those hills. Speaking of which, say 'Happy Birthday' to me the right way already!" Adele hugged me. I didn't want to let her go. "And it's true what they say," she said. "That you're only as old as you feel."

"How old do you feel?"

"About as old as I did when I used to roller skate on Hyde Street. I'd go down on my skates to the end of the block, and at the bottom it was like a slope and I would turn around and around. I was six. I can still feel it." Adele pointed to her heart. "Right here."

I could feel it, too. I thought of Adele's family. Did they ever know or hear their mother this way, or was she always and only "their mother." If they knew Adele, how could any child bear missing moments like this at the end of her parent's life?

Just then Fabian, from the front desk, came to the door with a package for Adele. I read off the box that it was from New Jersey. I got excited.

"That must be from my sister, Muriel!" Adele tried to sound matter-of-fact, like she was expecting the delivery all along.

"Cool!" I said. "A birthday gift! What a nice unexpected surprise!"

"I wonder what it is." Adele's voice got anxious. "Open it up and let's see. I bet it's my mother's prayer book. Muriel said she was going to send it to me so I could be buried with it."

"Now there's a thoughtful gift," I said, opening the box. "But this smells too good to be a book. It's a cake! A coffee cake!"

"A cake? I bet I know exactly where it comes from. Our *deeelicious* bakery in Newark. Now what was the name of that place? It was there even when Muriel and I were still young. Those were the days. Of course, Muriel is ten years younger than I am. She's my only sibling, you know. It was just her and me left. So what am I going to do with all of this cake?"

"Maybe you could share it with some people here," I suggested.

"The only one who cottons to me here is Mary," Adele said.

"What about Lorraine?" I asked. "When she wakes up. She might like a party, too."

"Well, we'll see who gets some of my cake and who doesn't." Adele tried to speak like a spoiled little brat. "Is there a card inside the cake? Tell me what it looks like so I can visualize it."

I told Adele the card had a cascade of lilacs coming out of a basket. Adele nestled close to me in her rocker. At ninety-four she could still enjoy hearing every word of a card.

"At the top of the card it says, 'For You, Sis.'"

"Oh, yes." Adele laughed to herself.

You could be ninety-four years old and still be somebody's "Sis." In that instant my heart felt young. The card was signed, "Take care of yourself. I love and miss you, Muriel."

"If your sister was here, she could have some of this cake," I said.

"Yes, and my daughter called this morning to wish me happy birthday, and so did my granddaughter."

"That's wonderful! See?" I was relieved. "You have a lot of love in your life."

"Well, yes, it's nice that they remember my birthday," Adele said sincerely. "But you're not going to leave now, are you? I like the flowers you brought me very much, too. My friendship with you is a separate feeling from family. This is an alive feeling. The other is there because it's just there. This is absolutely alive inside. I don't know how else to describe it."

In my lifetime I knew I would never again meet anyone who could describe it better. "I'm not leaving yet," I promised her.

"I told my daughter about our book and she said she looks forward to reading it, but I don't think she really believed me. Don't take this the wrong way," Adele said genteelly, "but sometimes your own family doesn't understand the things that happen in your life that are the most important."

"I know exactly what you mean." I held her hand. "But shall we go for a birthday stroll?"

Outside it was a perfect California day. Adele lifted her face to the sun. "Do you know what my birthday wish is?" Adele asked.

"Tell me."

"I wish that I will be here for my birthday next year."

"Amen." I laughed. "A-women, too."

"A-women, and how!" Adele laughed. "Did I ever tell you about the goldfish I got from my father for my birthday one year? I kept it in the bathtub! I had to always watch out that when anyone took a bath, they didn't let my fish go down the drain. Can you imagine?"

We went down to our bench under the tree.

"I want to send a nice note to Muriel," Adele said. "Do you have paper on you?"

"I'm sure I do. I've always got something."

"Then could you write it for me?"

"It would be my pleasure," I said. I scrambled through my purse for a pen.

Then Adele began to dictate.

Hi, Muriel,

    I think of you very often. And I was not surprised that YOU remembered MY birthday. Well, what do you expect? Age will tell. Just wait until you get there. Thanks so much for that lovely cake. I know where it came from even if you didn't tell me, and I'm going to enjoy this with my very best friend, Leah.

    The weather here is beautiful, but I know you will have to get your snow shovel out soon while we are sitting around a great big tree about a block away from the house enjoying a beautiful day. You most likely will be wallowing in snow but it's all right. You can throw a snowball for me. I always liked that kind of thing. Tonight, because it is my birthday, I will spend it out on the town. Dreamland is for me. Leah is writing this and laughing at me, but she's the one who is going to tell all the dirt about me when she finishes the book she's writing. Keep as well as you can and don't let Father Time get you down. Maybe one day you'll be able to sit down and open a book and read about all the bad things your sister did in her lifetime. Leah is writing this for me, of course. She knows if she doesn't do it, I'll pinch her.

    Always, with love,
    Your Sis.

PART THREE

A Coming of Aging

TIME IS ON ITS SIDE

It was one evening a few weeks later that I knew things with Adele had begun to change. I got a call from Joanna at the Chateau. It was supper time, and Adele hadn't been to the dining room for a meal all day. Fabian had just gone down to her room and found Adele upset and shaken like no one had ever seen her before. Adele's vital signs were perfect, but they didn't know what was the matter with her because she wouldn't talk to anyone. All she would do was listen to her talking watch.

"Maybe Adele would listen to you," Joanna said. "Could you come for a visit tomorrow?"

I sped over to the Chateau with my heart racing. I was in a hurry that night because of other plans, but it felt good to be needed. When I got to Adele's room, I could see that Adele had at least been well enough to dress herself nicely like she did every other day. She was not going to die. I was relieved and then I started to get annoyed. It was as if Adele didn't even know I was there. She was sitting on the edge of her bed with her talking watch held to her ear. She pushed the button on the watch. I sat down beside her.

"Listen to this!" Adele said, pushing the button for the tenth time in a row. I was not in a patient, good-listener mode. I had a half hour to be there, get home, and get dressed for a dinner date with an agent who I suspected was going to talk my ear off.

"It's 5:30 and thirty seconds," the man in the watch said.

"It's 5:30 in the heavens," Adele repeated. "That's what I hear. Isn't that what you hear?"

I didn't hear anything about "in the heavens." What I did hear was that the man's voice sounded different and faster, like maybe he'd had a sex-change operation, but the watch still seemed to be telling the right time.

"If it's telling the right time, then why do I keep hearing 'in the heavens'?" Adele wanted to know.

I wanted very much to be patient, but how was I supposed to know why Adele was hearing what she was hearing? How could a person who had lived that long expect someone to explain her experience to her as if ninety-four years still hadn't taught her that nobody could explain their own? All I wanted to know was that this was not the beginning of the end for Adele and why she wasn't eating. When I asked Adele, she hit the button on her watch again.

"It's 5:33," the watch said.

"In the heavens," Adele repeated. "Listen to this."

Suddenly I had a thought that chilled my bones. Maybe Adele really was hearing "in the heavens." What if I was about to tell Adele she just needed a new battery in her hearing aid, and meanwhile she was being briefed by angels inaudible to a human unless heaven happened to be your next stop? What if this was it and her watch was just being set ahead so she'd be on time for the next dimension? What if she was right and ready to go, and I was just a small, impatient, arrogant living person who couldn't understand? If this was "it," then this just had to be a mistake. Somebody had to fix it. I knew it sounded ridiculous, but Adele wasn't old enough to die. Her vital signs were perfect. This couldn't be her time. I hugged Adele tight. Then I suggested that maybe all she needed was for her watch to be repaired.

"But what if they can't fix it?" Adele asked. She couldn't stop touching her watch. I was stunned by how totally and completely present Adele was in that moment. She didn't care about what she looked like or what I thought about her or where I was going for my stupid dinner. She was losing someone again in her world, and she was not afraid to show she was scared to death of it. I didn't know what it was like to face losing your husband and your child and now to face losing a man you had on your wrist twenty-four hours a day for five years, especially when he was often the only person who ever talked to you. I had no way of really relating to the emotional connection of Adele's relationship to the watch, but when she hit the button again, I did know one thing for certain—I was ready for that relationship to be over.

"I think it's time to buy a new watch," I said.

"Do you think it's worth it?" Adele got nervous. "I mean at my age, how much time could I have left? These watches aren't cheap!"

Then Adele said something I never thought I would hear her say, and I didn't want to hear her say it. "If you were me," she asked, "what would you do?" In that instant Adele was no longer someone I could look up to. I was the adult on duty. Adele looked at me, waiting for my answer. If I were her, if I woke up one day and I was ninety-four and still questioning whether now was the right time to buy, what I would do was kill myself. I would finally know I had waited my whole life for the right time to buy when it was impossible to find a right time. I would know I had had a lifetime of being duped. In the beginning, when you were a child, you couldn't buy really expensive shoes because how long could a kid wear a really good shoe before she grew out of it? As a teenager it was not a good time to buy a high-quality coat because the time hadn't exactly come yet when you were fully grown and everyone knew you would spend more time in your life fully grown than growing. Seven and a half decades later, you ended up like Adele, so confused that you didn't know if you had enough time to make it worth your time to even know the time. But how could Adele know how much time she had left if she didn't have a watch to tell her how much time she was losing?

"You owe it to yourself to buy a new watch."

"I'd better not get a new watch," Adele announced. "I think it was eighty bucks when I got this one back then. How can I justify spending that kind of money today when it's going to cost me so much money to be flown back to New Jersey when I die? It's just a watch. I'm not going to die if I don't know exactly what time it is."

I was very glad to hear that. I hugged her good-bye.

The next day, I stopped by the Chateau after their dinner, and Adele was standing at the front desk. Her hair was messed up, and she was breathing heavy. It sounded as if she had a horrible cold. I had never seen her looking so sick, and it scared me.

"Is it seven o'clock yet?" Adele called to a nurse behind the desk. "I need my seven o'clock medicine, but I don't know what time it is."

When Adele realized I was there, she reached out for my hand. Her grip was weak and sweaty. "I'm so glad you're here," she said. "I've never been like this before in my life. Listen to this!" She pushed the button on her watch, but no voice came out.

"Sometimes it says something, and sometimes it doesn't."

"Do you think that maybe now is a good time to get a new watch?" I asked her gently.

"I think I'd better," she said, almost in tears. "It's just the most horrible feeling. I'm utterly alone. When I put my head out the door to ask somebody the time, wouldn't you know it, that's when nobody comes by. I know it may sound ridiculous being so upset," Adele said.

"It doesn't sound ridiculous at all," I said. "Do you want someone to call Dr. Campbell?"

"I'm not sick," Adele assured me. "It's just nerves. This is what happens when you're over ninety. The time comes when you don't take things so well."

"I know," I said. "I am ahead of my time."

Adele let me help her take off the watch. Her hand was trembling. "Take it with you," she said. "Call to order a new one. Tell them at the front desk, and my daughter will send a check. She has my money. The company is in New York. You can describe exactly what this one looks like. I don't care how much it costs. Of course, it might take them several days to get the watch to me. I don't know what I'll do. I can't live like this anymore. I just can't. I feel like I'm losing my mind. I don't know how I'll make it through another night."

"You will." I hugged Adele. Then I left the Chateau nervous that she wouldn't make it. I knew even if I could find a temporary talking watch that night it wouldn't matter because in a half hour Adele would go to bed. She wouldn't need a watch while she was sleeping, although I couldn't imagine going to sleep without a clock by my bed to tell me how much time I had left to sleep every time I woke up. I comforted myself by recalling that huge parts of the world lived without paying any attention to time. They lived free like children. If it was dark, it was nighttime, and if it was light, it was daytime. The problem was as far as Adele knew, since she couldn't see, it could be nighttime in the middle of the afternoon. This could be the longest night of Adele's life.

At about 12:30, when I had turned off *David Letterman* and was ready to go to sleep, I took Adele's watch out of my purse and put it next to the phone by my bed so I could remember to call New York when I woke up. Off Adele's wrist, the watch looked different— more masculine and free. I pushed the button.

"It's 12:48," the man said. His voice sounded almost back to normal and deeper. It felt strange having Adele's guy by my bed since I had never even had Adele in my house. It seemed as if the watch had just faked not working for Adele so it could have a night away off-duty and see what it was like out in the real world. I had to get up and put the watch in my bathroom. The house and the neighborhood were unusually still, and I was about to hit the lights when I heard talking.

"It's 1:62," the voice said. "It's 1:62 P.M."

By the time I got into the bathroom the watch was telling time with a Liverpool accent. "It's 1:90, 1:90," he repeated. "1:90." I tossed a wash cloth over the watch but it didn't make the voice softer. It just got him angry.

"Attention!" the voice commanded. "Attention!" I ran over to my bed to get my flashlight. If I had to, I would smash the watch to death with it. I was mildly amused, but that was because I knew it was too late to call any of my friends for help and 911 seemed out of the question.

"It's 2:67 P.M.," the man said. I pressed down hard on the button, but the voice wouldn't let up. "It's 2:67 A.M. and P.M.," the voice snapped.

I flashed on years earlier when I was in my twenties and alone in my apartment when a raccoon went into convulsions at my front door. He looked so sweet and helpless. "Don't touch it," the man from Animal Control hollered at me over the phone. "I've seen a raccoon chomp through a billy club in one bite. Can you imagine what that thing will do to your hand?"

Now it was too late. I was holding the watch up to my ear by its band and shaking it. The watch was laughing and telling the time in Angola, and then it turned nasally and sputtered out seconds backwards and then finally—silence. I looked at the clock by my bed. It was 1:11. Adele's watch was dead. I got into bed and had a horrible feeling that Adele had died at exactly the same time, 1:11. I had heard about these things happening. I couldn't stop visualizing Adele alone in that room. What a horrible, unfair way for a person to die. I wasn't ready to face losing her. By four o'clock, I was knocking myself out with Advil to fall asleep.

I woke up at nine and went directly to Radio Shack. They had two talking watches—one with a rooster that crowed before a different barnyard animal told the time, and the other that sounded like Mae West sucking on helium.

I found Adele in her room in her rocking chair listening to a talking book. She looked a little better than she had the night before, but she still sounded shaky. She told me she only made it through the night because Lorraine let her sleep with her radio on the station that told the freeway report and the time every six minutes.

"What time is it?" Adele asked.

I took Mae West out of the bag and played it for Adele. "It's 10:22," Mae said.

"Don't worry," I told Adele. "She's temporary."

"I understand," Adele said, feeling around for the button on the new watch. Mae was more complicated than Adele's old watch.

"What time is it?" Adele asked. "I know you just told me how to work this thing, but at my age I'm entitled to forget things. I have to remember my age. I just have to be patient. It bothers me that consciously and subconsciously a watch means that much to me, but it does. Nothing like this ever happened to me before. I was always so responsible for my own life. Now I feel helpless. Nobody escapes Father Time. I'm just trying to be realistic and face the facts," Adele said, feeling for my hand. "And now that's what I want you to do, too."

I felt embarrassed, as if I had been caught in the act of still being a child. I *was* facing facts. The fact was that we could live without time. And no matter how much time Adele lived, never was going to be the right time for her to die. Period.

THE GHOST OF
CHRISTMAS FUTURE

Three days before Christmas, I told Adele I would be there at two o'clock to take her to the Chateau Christmas party. When it came time, I really did not want to go, but I had missed the one other program they had for the season. It was a support group for residents and their families on ways to beat holiday depression, which was an obvious success for the families since not a one of them was at the party today. I was the only person in the room from "the outside."

"I couldn't do it," my friend Eva had said earlier. "Especially at Christmas. It's hard enough going to see my mother at her apartment. I just hope I'm dead before I get that old. But worst case scenario, if we're all still around, we won't be spending Christmas in an old people's home. We'll organize a seniors' society somewhere in Cabo San Lucas," Eva said, which sounded like a stretch to me since it took from one to three months now for us to organize meeting for dinner.

Now the activities director was leading the group in "You'd better not pout, you'd better not cry," and Adele was singing the way she liked to—loud. She didn't care what people thought. If there was a party, she was going to sing—even if wasn't "her holiday." Now everybody was looking at her. I had been coming to the Chateau so often that nobody looked at me like I was young and special anymore. I wasn't. I was just some younger person who wasn't sharp enough to go out and have a life before I really had to live in a place like this. Today I was a regular, old and stuck. I wasn't nervous about losing Adele anymore. I was more afraid she could live well into her hundreds. I had to pace myself. I couldn't subject myself to every Christmas party that came along in this place.

Of the parties I had been to at the Chateau, this one was the most packed and the most deadly. The Alzheimer's residents were there and staring at their hands. A man slid out of his seat and had to be lifted up off the floor by two nurses. There was a definite smell of urine that you didn't get at the other parties.

"Excuse me, miss," a man said in a wheelchair next to me. "Am I bleeding?" He showed me his wrists, covered with blood as if he had just tried to slit them on the spoke of his wheelchair.

"Yes, you are," I tried to say calmly. Then I flagged down an orderly.

The activities director turned on a cassette of Christmas carols to lead the group, and there was a choir of people singing on the tape. Adele was thrilled.

"It's different because they don't have outside entertainment, but it's nice," Adele said. "I don't care that they're Christmas carols. This is the first time I've actually heard everyone singing! And you know, they don't sound half-bad. Do you think?"

I was trying not to. I didn't have the heart to tell Adele what was really going on. Then, when a man came in delivering a ten-pound gift bag of caramel corn for a resident with three teeth, I knew I didn't have what it was going to take to make it all the way through this party. Even if it only lasted one hour. I had to have a break. I told Adele I'd be back in a minute, and I got up to go hang out in the bathroom. One of the residents tapped me on the shoulder to point out that as I was leaving, I was walking directly under the mistletoe. Before I could turn my cheek, he kissed me on the mouth. I was now heading for the bathroom with a purpose.

I discovered that the maintenance crew had blocked off the hallway that led to the visitors' bathroom, and the woman at the desk told me the only way I could get there now was to go through the Green Garden. The Green Garden was the last place Adele ever wanted to go, and I didn't want to go there by myself now, but I didn't want to walk back into the party yet, either.

The Green Garden was where the last hope/second-level Alzheimer's patients stayed. There wasn't a speck of green in the place. Everything was sky blue with fluffy white clouds so as to give the impression that you were somewhere over the rainbow—somewhere where you didn't have to remember you had forgotten everything. It was perfectly still back there, and even though nobody was around, all the doors to the rooms were wide open so I could look inside. They were much bigger and better appointed than the rooms in the retirement section where Adele lived and not much unlike the room I shared with my sister when we were growing up. Only here there were no posters of The Beatles and the beds were perfectly made. Somehow I could see a Christmas forty years down the road. I would find myself living in a room like this again without a single memory of this day when I swore I was still a little girl, just passing through trying to find her way to the bathroom.

I was eighty-five years old then. I could not visualize myself, but I knew I looked pretty much the same, only shorter. I was a widow and on my own, but I was not all alone. There were plenty of other people my age around, but I couldn't see any faces clearly enough to tell if any of them were my lifetime friends. If it was them, they looked different and terribly old. My mind was sharp, and the only kind of severe mental loss I had was I could not remember my nieces were not coming for Christmas but had a fruitcake delivered instead. Life was not bad.

Like all other days, on Christmas there were planned activities. I was pushing my walker down to the room where the sing-along was starting. I was flashing on years back when I went to the sing-alongs with Adele. I could still recall how those old, despondent people came back to life when they sang the songs from their own generation, like all the Irving Berlins and "God Bless America." That day we would be singing "In a Gadda-Da-Vida," the long version.

During the drum solo, I was getting up and going to the game room. We were the first generation of old people that didn't have our own functional old people's game. Nobody could remember enough to play "Trivial Pursuit." Some people were reading the obituaries from the newspaper and playing "Guess Who Died." I was knowing that game was really from our parent's generation, but now people were playing the baby boomer's edition—"Guess Who Had a Near Death," "Guess Who Died and Came Back," "Guess Who Tried to E-mail You from 'The Other Side.'" Death was much easier. I was attending all of my funerals on-line. A woman with children was waiting for them to show up and take her out for a Christmas dinner. The rest of us were taking out photos of our long-deceased dogs and talking about how unnatural it was for a parent to outlive her children.

I was in the first of the oldest generation alive in history. My generation had already lived twice as long as our grandparents and were twice as healthy as my parents. I was going off to have my regular checkup. I was remembering Adele and how she waited in line for Dr. Campbell. Once a month Dr. Campbell would come to the Chateau with his white pad and fire off prescriptions for all the residents. Sometimes he would check first to see that they had a pulse. Now, years later, I was reminiscing how primitive it was for them then to entrust their health to one doctor. I was in line first to see the Chinese doctor and the Ayurvedic doctor, the aromatherapist, the color therapist, the magnets therapist, the gastroenterologist, the rheumatologist, and my psychic gynecologist. My future looked good, as long as I didn't run out of money.

In the afternoon I was sitting out on the patio and looking at my bankbook. I was recalling the Chateau where Adele lived had cost her $800 a month and that the top price for medical care there was $2,000. I was remembering that was just an average price for an average old person's place at the turn of the millennium. Now I was making my payment to the California Condo for $20,000. I was lucid enough not to be expecting the Social Security check to come in the mail. I was aware I had few of the retirement benefits my parents or Adele's generation had. What I had inherited from my generation was the inner child's knowledge that I would be taken care of. I was still in the majority generation. We could not be ignored because we were like pigeons. We were seventy million strong. We did not have to worry about our future. The generation of Attention Deficit Disorder was responsible for the Alzheimer's generation. They were providing. Those of us with exceptionally wealthy children were living in seniors' condos in the Caribbean. The rest of us were the new, old middle class. We had seen the youngsters reconvert the defunct malls into senior housing. Now we were living in the old malls. This room of mine was on the first floor. I was spending the last years of my life in The Limited.

My heart started pounding. Then I realized I was not in some wretched mall. I was still in the Alzheimer's Garden almost running down another blue corridor looking for the way out. Rapture! I was still young enough to find it. There was a double door ahead with a sign on it that said:

ATTENTION GREEN GARDEN RESIDENTS—ALARM WILL SOUND IF YOU OPEN THE DOOR WITHOUT PRIOR AUTHORIZATION.

That sign was not for me. I pushed the door. An alarm went off. I flashed on a terrifying science fiction film classic from the late seventies, *Logan's Run,* set in a world of the future where the law stated that everyone had to die when they turned thirty. Some "old" people tried to get face-lifts to look younger or just run from the police, but the "runners" never got away. They had to die. I was not a runner. Clearly anybody could see that I was not a Garden resident. Everything we baby boomers said should happen to old people in the seventies didn't happen. The way of the world was different now. Age was no longer the enemy. Hadn't anyone heard? I was forty-five and still cool.

Just then I saw an orderly coming down the other end of the hallway, and I froze. He had on big baggy pants, and his eyebrows were pierced so as to make it obvious he was pushing twenty-five. He punched up a bunch of numbers on a panel and made the alarm stop. I told the orderly I was just trying to get back to the party—in a way that made me sound like "real people." He said if I liked this party, I should come back on New Year's Eve.

"They have some punch, blow some noisemakers, take their medication, and pass out by eight o'clock. It's hilarious." He laughed.

"Old people know how to par-tay. You know what I'm talking about?"

Of course I knew what he was talking about. I had been par-tay-ing like that for a decade. But I wasn't about to make fun of that just to let him see I was all right. He didn't deserve to know yet how truly bitchin' it could be to have a friendship with someone fifty years older than you. He didn't have to know that just because he wore those big, baggy pants that made him look like he was carrying a load didn't mean he got to be a baby forever. He didn't need to know yet that the trick to New Year's Eve was to keep a dress in the closet for hope and peace in your heart that wherever or whoever you were with when the ball ultimately dropped in Times Square was out of your hands. This kid didn't need to know how good it could be. All I needed him to do was let me out the door. I had to get back to Adele. I knew then the key to ensuring my future was to par-tay now. Not just because later would be too late, but because later I wouldn't know how to party any better than I let myself party now. No matter where I lived.

When I got back to the party, Adele was chewing a Fig Newton and belting out "White Christmas."

"I'm glad you're here." She reached for my hand. "I was afraid you left to run off and get married."

"Not exactly," I said.

"What's the matter? Isn't he persistent enough? Do you want me to talk to him?"

"I want you to create him." I laughed. "He doesn't exist."

"Well, keep your eyes open," Adele said. "You're not going to be twenty-nine forever. The perfect man could be right under your nose and you don't know it. I'll help you find him. Although he probably isn't in a place like this."

"Hopefully not."

"I was just thinking," Adele said, "if I could have anything for Christmas, what it would be."

"What?"

"I would just wish that there wasn't such a tremendous age difference between you and me."

"Why is that?"

"Because if I was closer to your age, I could go out with you one day, and we could have some real fun. I could do some of the things that you like to do for a change," Adele said, holding my hand tight.

"This is it." I laughed, popping another Fig Newton into Adele's mouth. "You're looking at it."

True Friends

The first Monday of the new year I was doing my last lap around the park with Bob when something happened that stopped me in my tracks. Bob asked me out. I tried to tell him I was flattered but afraid of ruining the great friendship we had inside the park since I was certain we were going to have nothing in common outside of it.

"You're right," Bob agreed. "We probably don't have a thing in common except you're not seeing anybody and I'm not seeing anybody and we both have to eat. So I'd like to take you out for a nice dinner. What's the worst thing that could happen? God forbid you should have a good time. How bad could that be?"

I didn't know, but I said Friday night I'd be willing to find out. I had four days to get out of this.

"Only four more days." Bob laughed. "You're not going to try to weasel your way out of this, are you?"

"If I didn't want to go out with you, I would have told you so," I tried to say with authority.

Nobody but Bob knew how important my walks in the park were. I had never mentioned there was a Bob to anyone other than

Jenny. Now Jenny was out of town, and I was too embarrassed to talk this over with any of my other girlfriends since they saw me as skilled on first dates, and they might not understand the potential problem with this one. If something went sour with Bob, I would lose my friend and my track. Bob walked me to my car like he always did. Then, on my way home, I found myself driving to Adele's for a surprise visit.

"You must have heard my brains moving," Adele said when she came to her door. "I was just thinking about you."

"What were you thinking?"

"I was thinking how much I enjoy our visits. I've met a lot of people in my day and after all these years, I've never met a person like you. I hope I never lose you."

"Why would you lose me?" I was taken aback. "Why? Do you want me to get lost?"

"Of course not. You're all I've got! But maybe I could become a nuisance to you." I could tell Adele was afraid of not pleasing me.

"You're my friend," I said. "I think about you all the time, even when I'm not here."

"After all these years I finally have a true friend," Adele said sincerely.

"Really?" I was stunned. "You mean you never had close girl-friends?"

"Only women to go out to lunch with," Adele said. "But we never talked near this way. And the tremendous difference in our ages and lives doesn't seem to make any difference at all."

"I know what you mean," I said. "You're my most remarkable friend."

"Well, I'm not a fair-weather friend." Adele smiled. Then she felt for my hand. "What's the matter?" she said. "You seem as if something is wrong. There's not a life that has all good days. Tell me what's bothering you. Are you in trouble?"

"It's nothing serious," I assured her, "but I think I need some advice. I've been walking with this guy for almost three years. He's become a good friend. And now I think he may be kind of cute, and he wants to take me out for dinner."

"Should I be happy for you?"

"If you'd like," I said.

"If you'd like, I'd like," Adele said lovingly. "I have no right to have any feeling because I'm not concerned. It's for you to step back and look at with open eyes. You have to have the feeling for the person and then back off and look item by item. Is he college educated? What does he do to earn his keep?"

"He's a construction worker," I said reluctantly.

"That's all?" Adele stopped cold.

In that instant I had to remember not to resent Adele for the difference between our generations. If I had delivered this same information to a girlfriend, she would have said, "Construction worker? At least he must have good hands."

"Well, he may be naturally intelligent without the diploma," Adele finally said. "Whereby the educated one may be educated so highly that he picks every item apart. I just want the best for you. I feel for you as if you were my own."

I kissed Adele on the cheek and held her hand tight. It had been a long time since I had been anybody's own, and it felt good. Then I thought of Bob. I thought maybe I could be his own. Until I saw him again Wednesday in the park.

"Looking forward to Friday?" Bob fished.

"What's Friday?" I asked. "Do you really think this is such a good idea?"

"Sure it is," Bob said without hesitation. "Well, that is if we're having sushi. Is six o'clock too late?"

Was this guy kidding? Six o'clock was perfect! That way we could eat at the same time as Adele.

I went back to see her before my date on Friday.

"I've been thinking," Adele said, "when you see your friend, you'll want to find out: Is he kind? Is he friendly, cooperative, and willing? Is he the type who always has to be right?"

"I already know those things about him," I said. "I just have no idea what he looks like sitting down. I've only seen him when we're walking!"

"Has he been married?" Adele wanted to know. I told her Bob had been divorced a year longer than me, and Adele wanted to know why the marriage hadn't worked out.

"His wife cheated on him."

"Have you verified this?" Adele was as good at this kind of questioning as Jenny.

"We're friends," I reminded her. "We're going out for dinner. I'm not getting married."

"Well, yes, just to be friends you don't have to dig down deep to verify every account." Adele sounded relieved. "And you can tell him I said that as a friend you cannot be improved on. Who knows? He might catch you off guard just at the right moment. Never in my life would I have dreamed that God would put me in this hellhole. And then he gave me a friend like you just when I needed it. And I was thinking"—Adele lifted her head to the ceiling—"how someone who was at first unknown has turned out to be utterly different from all the people I've ever known."

"Back at you," I said, which was the best I could do at saying I was embarrassed by the beauty of what she had just said. I had never had a friend talk to me like that.

"God gives us just what we need, not what we want, and He gives it to us just when we need it."

I took Adele's words as a sign from God that He was about to give me something good. I left excited.

Then I went off to meet Bob. As soon as I saw him in the restaurant, I knew God wasn't going to give me what I wanted, and if this was what I needed, I didn't want it. After dinner we drove in my car to walk where there was a lake and no lights, and halfway around the path we sat down on a bench and kissed. Kissing Bob was like kissing a friendly piece of cardboard.

I drove Bob back to his car at the restaurant and I felt disappointed, but we were completely goofy and we laughed hard all the way. I said I suspected we were not meant to be more than friends, and we agreed that we'd meet up at the park the next day. I went to sleep looking forward to that. Then starting the next day, Bob stopped showing up.

I thought about everything Adele had said. She was right. God gives us just what we need. I did not need a construction worker.

CAN I LIVE WITH YOU?

"I hope I don't have to spend too many more years like this in a place like this," Adele told me one depressing afternoon a few weeks later.

"I know what you mean," I said.

"I can't sit in this room anymore," Adele went on. "It's utterly lonely. I just hope that nothing like this ever happens to you and you end up living in a place like this."

I didn't have the heart to tell Adele that that day I felt like I already had.

"Tomorrow will be better." I tried to buoy both of us up. "It's your day to go to the Seniors' Center. That's something you look forward to."

"*Look forward* is a little strong." Adele tried to chuckle. "I just go from sitting here blind like a dope to sitting there like a dope. Besides, I don't think I'm even going to go tomorrow."

"Why not?" I got frightened that Adele was about to cut herself off from her only outside activity besides me.

"The van that they use to drive us back here at the end of the day makes me feel nauseous. Last time I didn't think I was going to make it home without dropping dead first."

"Why don't you take the van that goes in the morning tomorrow, and at the end of the day I'll come pick you up," I heard myself offer.

"You will?" Adele seemed genuinely surprised. "But you're busy."

"It will be my pleasure. Besides, I'm just sitting at home writing about you all day. I might as well take time out and come get you. It gives me a little variation on a theme. A change of pace is good for both of us," I assured her.

"Well, yes." Adele's face lit up. "And, of course, if you come for me I will be the only one there who doesn't have to go home in the van. Tomorrow will be better."

The next day when I went to pick up Adele, she was outside smiling as if she knew all the old people boarding the vans were watching her drive off in my car.

"There's a new woman who sits at my table, and she lives with her son," Adele told me.

"How nice!" I said, like a mother listening to my child report on her day at school.

"She was telling everyone the son says he'll never get married until she dies. Doesn't that sound good?"

"Good?" I just about jumped out of my skin. "That sounds horrible! Why should he give up his life like that? Besides, you think it's so great being that woman? Her son is probably out working all day, and she has to sit in the house waiting by herself."

"Well, I suppose you're right," Adele said. "But you don't have to leave your house to go to work. And that gave me an idea of something I wanted to ask you," Adele said as I pulled into the Chateau driveway, "and I realize it's no small question." Adele stopped for a second to gather her strength. "But can I live with you? I was figuring that way neither of us would have to live so alone. I'm independent even though I'm blind. I think I could still fix a nice salad. I haven't seen your place yet, but if it's just a matter of needing more space, I could pitch in. I get my Social Security check, you know. I can talk straight with you because we're real friends," Adele said without hesitation. "But you don't have to give me your answer today because I'm sure with something like this you'd want to think it over a little."

I helped Adele out of the car as if there were nothing out of line about her request. Of course she couldn't live with me. But I was in shock. Right now the only sentence I could string together was "You realize, Adele, I'm not home all the time, either."

"It would still be better for me than living in this place," Adele pleaded. "Can I just come and sit with you while you write?"

"I have to be alone when I write," I was able to say clearly.

"I understand." Adele backed off. "It's just that I miss you. I can't help it if you're someone who is easy to miss. Nobody thinks they're going to end up like this when they're a hundred percent and busy. You can't expect them to. But things don't remain a bed of roses. The roses wither and die." Adele's voice got desperate. "So what are you going to do the rest of the afternoon, honey?"

What did she think I was going to do? I was going to go with her to her room like I always did and tell her what day I'd be back like I always did. And then, when I heard her door click behind me, I was going to do a fast walk down the hallway and then run for my life. The worst had happened to Adele. She had turned a corner of old age where she now thought she had the right to ask for anything she wanted.

I got into my car and revved up the engine. I was going to burn rubber pulling out of that driveway. I didn't need Adele scheming up ways for me to not live alone. We were not the Bobsey Twins. I wasn't a lonely old lady like she was. I could still get somebody to miss me. I was still young enough to be rock and roll, and right now I needed to burn off steam. So I headed for a walk in the park. In the back of my mind I hoped that Bob might be there walking for the first time since our date. I could tell him what a jerk he had been for not coming back there sooner. He would explain himself, and I would realize he was still a good man. We could be friends again, and I'd tell him this latest escapade about Adele and he would make me laugh. My heart started to pound.

It was the very start of rush hour, and I figured if I drove to the freeway fast enough, I'd be out on the track in fifteen minutes. I made a turn and pulled onto the entrance of the freeway just in time to watch a Bunny Bread truck drive into the back of a new Porsche. Now I wasn't going anywhere. Six lanes of traffic came to a dead halt.

I thought of Adele at that moment in her rocking chair day-dreaming about the good life she would have if only she could live with me.

I didn't want to be chained to a woman who wasn't even my mother. I had already done that with my own mother ten years ago. I had held her in my arms and looked inside her blackened-out mouth while she cried out in pain like a dying wolf because cancer was trampling through her body. I had already flown back to Chicago because my father drove to the store to get his medicine, and when he came out, he couldn't remember where he had parked his car or how to call a cab or my sister. So he walked five hours in the dark and cold trying to find his way home with no one stopping to help him when he cried out he was lost. I wasn't going to feel sorry for Adele because she couldn't move her bowels at ninety-four when my friend Betsy had Parkinson's and couldn't move her arms at forty-three.

Did it once cross your mind, Adele, that all you would really get with me was bumper-to-bumper traffic on the Hollywood freeway and a track you could walk around on like a hamster with some guy named Bob who probably wasn't even going to be there because he wasn't ever really your friend to begin with? Was the good life starting to sound like hell to you? Would you turn on me like Bob did because I didn't give you the answer that you wanted?

Or should I just come to my senses and move you in with me for the rest of your life? Should I promise not to marry until you die? Should I beg your forgiveness because I am not selfless and I am not Mother Theresa and I don't want to give you one more inch than what I'm giving you now because I don't even have it to give? Do you want to tell the adoption agency that sent me to you in the first place that they made a mistake and they should hurry up and send somebody decent? Go ahead, call them. See if I care!

The next thing I knew I was turning off the freeway and heading back for Adele's. I couldn't wait until tomorrow to talk to her. If I got to her room fast enough, I could get this over with and be out the door before Adele had to go for her dinner.

I got to the Chateau at twenty minutes after five, just in time to see Adele locking up her room so she could start down to the dinner time lineup. She reached in her purse to get her foldable cane. I watched her fiddling to open it. Every small act was a commitment to go on, and somehow this woman made it through. I ran down the hallway to help her.

"Oh, my God, I was wishing you were here, and here you are." Adele squeezed my hand in disbelief. I could tell she had been upset. "I was thinking," Adele said.

"Me, too." I took Adele's arm. "That's why I came back here. What have you been thinking?"

"I was thinking I don't know what they're going to have that I can eat for dinner. Mary said she heard we're having some kind of chicken breasts, but she didn't tell me this until half an hour ago and by then it was already too late to try and find somebody to order me something else in the kitchen." Adele stopped to catch her breath. "They say you have to do that by one o'clock. I can't eat white meat chicken because it's terrible here. It's too dry and it makes me gag. And of course nobody's going to listen to me because I'm blind. I can't just try to find my way into the kitchen and ask them to make me a peanut butter sandwich!"

"I can," I heard myself say. "Would you like me to do that for you?"

"Would you?" Adele's face lifted. "Do I have to tell you I thank God for you? Now I know why He sent you back to me just now. Isn't it remarkable how God has certain things work?"

Yes, it was. But I still had to tell Adele the truth.

A man with thick, huge glasses walked right up to me the way he did to everybody. "Did you hear the joke about the pregnant baseball? She got all knocked up in the stands. Get it?" He breathed in my face.

"Who was that?" Adele asked.

"Robin Williams." I made Adele walk faster.

"Hi, Adele," a woman called out when we reached the end of the lineup. "It's nice you have your daughter with you so much."

"That's not her daughter," the warthog corrected her. "She just takes Adele for walks."

"You're the girl who picked up Adele from the Seniors' Center today in a sports car!" A man who looked like Jimminy Cricket dropped his mouth open like he was having a celebrity citing. Everyone stared at me. Then the big thick lineup seemed to part down the middle to let us through.

"I need to talk to you about something you asked before," I tried to whisper.

"Of course," she assured me. "I didn't forget. When you go back there in the kitchen, ask them if they would just please make me a sandwich with a little bread and something else. If they don't have any peanut butter, it can be just plain toast. That would be fine. You can just tell them it's for me. Of course, I don't have to tell you what to say," Adele corrected herself. "You know how to open your mouth."

"I'll be right back." I started for the kitchen.

"Don't worry," Mary said, "I'll stand right here with her."

"She's a nice girl," I heard someone else saying to Adele. "You're lucky to have a friend."

"Oh, yes," Adele said too loudly. "She's a lovely person. She's just going to get me something special for dinner."

Now I was alone trying to find my way for the first time behind the scenes through the kitchen and over to the hairnet people who spoke very little English. The answer was hot dogs. The best they could do back there was a hot dog on a bun.

I got back to Adele just as the lineup started moving. "A hot dog is fine," Adele said. "Of course, you know what they call a hot dog here is not what I'd call a hot dog. They're not Jewish."

"How do you know that?" I was trying hard not to sound too sarcastic. "They're not circumcised?"

"That's right." Adele laughed. We reached the dining room doors. I could hardly wait to drop her off and get out of there. I would have to tell her tomorrow that my answer was no.

"I have to go in now with Mary," Adele said. "Do you want to come eat with me at my table? The food is not so bad here, you know."

"That's okay," I told her. "I'm going to go home."

"You mean you have to go and start cooking dinner for yourself now?" Adele sounded concerned.

"It's fine," I promised.

"It's too bad you have to eat alone," Adele said. "I'm glad I don't have that here." Then Adele kissed me good-bye and walked as fast as she could to her table.

I stood there stunned. The truth was I was eating alone. I was going for my walk and then home to make pea soup, and I was angry. I went back to my car, picked up the phone, and called Bob.

"Is there any particular reason why you stopped coming to the park for the first time right after we went out?" I asked him.

"I was disappointed, it's true," Bob said. "But then I decided I needed a change from walking in the park. I just needed a change of scenery. A change of pace is good."

"Are you changing your friends, too?"

"We're still friends," Bob said. "I still have the same feelings for you, I'm just not going to pursue you. You know, life is short."

"So am I," I said. "And if we're still going to be friends, I need to talk once in a while."

"No problem," Bob said. "Want to meet me at the park?"

"No problem."

I drove over to the park and we walked. We walked for a very long time. Then when we got done with that, Bob took me out for sushi. Somehow this time dinner was utterly different than it was a few weeks ago. Our relationship was about to change forever.

One Age Fits All

"How's it going with the guy?" Jenny asked me from her car phone about a month later. "Have you looked inside his refrigerator yet?"

"Why?" I asked. "Was I supposed to?"

"That's what I did when I was still single," Jenny said. "If I was starting to get serious about somebody, I'd check to see 'Does this guy have anything real to eat, or is there just mold and a beer in there?' Trust me." Jenny emphasized her point. "You can tell a lot about how mature a guy is by seeing what's going on in the inside of his refrigerator."

"I'll take a look," I assured Jenny. I didn't have the courage to tell her that so far I had only checked out the back cabin of Bob's truck. We were parking in the parking lot after hours, laughing and making out like teenagers.

"Hey, I've got an idea," Jenny called back the next day. "Your birthday is coming up. When was the last time you even threw a party? I can't remember!"

Neither could I. But I was embarrassed enough now that I knew I was going to have one this year.

"It doesn't have to be anything big," Jenny said. "Just the family—you know, the immediate close friends. Then everybody can check out the guy. And can you bring the old lady? I'm dying to meet her, too! Oh, I think that sounds like it will be so much fun!"

So much fun? Had Jenny ever tried entertaining someone over ninety? I felt guilty because right now I was the worst kind of fickle friend to Adele, but having her at my party did not sound like fun. Bob was fun. He was the most childlike adult friend I had ever had. Fun was buying a Ouija board with Bob and asking it what numbers to pick to win that night's super lotto. That was the kind of question Adele was never going to ask at a party.

"I wonder what do they do with people's things when they die here?" Adele asked me the next day when I got to her room. She seemed unusually soft-spoken. She was alone in there and her roommate Lorraine's bed looked neat as if it hadn't been slept in.

"If the person dies and she doesn't have next of kin," Adele wanted to know, "do they give their things to the indigents who otherwise wouldn't have anything?"

I knew something was wrong and this was a very real question to Adele's world now, but if only she could have heard how surreal it sounded to me when I had pâté decisions to make for my party.

"I don't know what they do," I said. "Do you want me to find out?"

I found out Lorraine had been taken to the hospital again in the middle of the night, and now Adele didn't know for sure if she was coming back. She was frightened, and she did not like spending all that time alone in there in the dark. I couldn't help but throw my arms around her.

"Of course when I die, I do have next of kin," Adele went on. "They'll see to it that my belongings go to my daughter or my sister

Muriel. Muriel and I are going to be buried in the same cemetery in New Jersey. I have a double space next to my husband."

"That sounds nice," I said.

"Of course, they'll have to remove the stone to let me in."

"That sounds right," I said. I was anxious to flip this conversation shut.

"We bought a plot for Muriel because she was divorced and she'll be next to me, and then there's one plot left for Muriel's daughter if she wants it, because she's an old maid and this way she won't be dead alone."

"It's good to have a plan."

"Absolutely," Adele said. Then she stopped and looked at me like she was about to ask a very important question. "You're going to have a funeral, aren't you?"

"I don't know," I said. "I'm not going to be there. Would it be okay if we talked about something else today?"

"Of course." Adele understood. "I hope you're putting away money now, little by little, for when you die. You're not going to be twenty-nine forever. Have you thought about how much 'do-re-me' it costs to fly a corpse back on an airplane?"

I had no idea. But I did know no matter how much somebody paid me, I wasn't going to have Adele talking corpses at my house. I knew then why people put their parents in these places. It was for their parents' own protection so their children wouldn't kill them when they wanted to have a party. Nobody wanted to have the constant reminder in their face that the older you got, the more kindness and patience your life was going to require.

Two days later I could barely get myself back to Adele's like I said I would. I couldn't bear to hear anymore about the arrangements for Adele's funeral, and I wasn't ready to casket shop for mine.

"Whistle so I can find you," Adele called when I walked into her room. Lorraine was back from the hospital and in bed. "That's all she does is sleep. There's nobody here to help me," Adele blurted out in frustration. Then she gave herself to the count of five to snap out of it. "One—two—three—four—five. Good. That's enough. Come here and give me a kiss." Adele reached for my cheek. "I'm so glad to see you." Her face was filled with light. "How do you feel?"

Like scum. I had forgotten the courage and love Adele brought forth just to make it through every simple action of her life, blind and on her own in this room. She was truly wonderful.

"You don't stay as long anymore because you don't want to." Adele caught me off guard. "Is that because you're spending all your time with the carpenter?"

"You mean Bob? The construction worker? I'm not just with him all the time," I said. "I'm working and I'm still here with you more than an hour a week."

"You give me an hour?" Adele asked. "How much are you charging me an hour?"

"I don't know. How much have you got?"

"I'm sorry." Adele backed off. "I've loved you from the beginning. I don't know why. How many people will go out of their way to help others like you do? You remind me of myself when I could still do, and I mean really do for others." Adele's voice started to crack. "Did I ever tell you I volunteered for the Red Cross? I bathed a man who was crippled and I visited the blind. I wasn't afraid of somebody because they were handicapped or old. I still feel good when I just think back about it. You'll see." Adele rubbed her eyes under her glasses. Then she stopped talking and she cried like she was trying with all her might to let tears come out. "I didn't think I could still cry at this age. Oh, God," she called out. "Give me strength!"

I held Adele's hand. I could not see a single tear rolling down Adele's cheek. I was not running to get her a Kleenex. I did not feel afraid to just sit there. That's what girlfriends did for each other.

"Doing for others is what makes life worth it." Adele gathered her composure. "And you can't buy that. You have to earn it. Some people think they can live for themselves. But as the end begins to come clear, their minds work in the past and they really get thinking. I wonder what they think they could have done or not done just by doing a little for others. But then it's too late."

Adele and I sat side by side in her chairs, and for me it was as if time was standing still. There was nowhere else in the world I had to go.

"It may sound ridiculous, but I wish I could still go out and volunteer today. Even if all I had to offer was to show that if I can do what I'm doing at my age, they could do it, too."

"You have a lot to offer." I smiled. "You've changed my life."

"I love you as if you were my own." Adele hugged me. "And, of course, I think you deserve the best. That's why I just don't want to see you rush into anything and fall into a ditch you can't get out of with some uneducated man."

"Marriage, eloquently put," I said, hoping Adele would catch I was jarred into sarcasm. Then I was overcome with the instinct to be patient. "Don't worry," I assured her. "Even if I were to ever get re-married, you would still and always be in my life."

But exactly forty-three minutes from then, when my hour was up, I was out the door. It was okay that I didn't say a word to Adele about my party. If I wanted old people there, I could have rented out the Chit Chat Room. Even Bob, who was a Vietnam combat vet, told me he wanted to meet Adele, but he was afraid of the way old people could smell. The last thing I needed was to have Adele at my house smelling, and insulting Bob because he didn't have a college degree. I had my hands full with just worrying about my friends meeting Bob.

*   *   *

The day before my birthday I drove to Adele's, promising myself I would stay only ten minutes, since I knew I wouldn't be able to take any more time than that. I felt guilty. I was setting this up to be the beginning of the end of Adele by turning this into a perfunctory "old lady" visit. I assured myself I was doing the best I could under the circumstances; I was not going to be manipulated into even more guilt by this woman. Once I got past my party, things would get back to normal.

When I got to Adele's room, she was ready and waiting to go for a walk. I told her I didn't have long so we started for a stroll down the hallway. Adele asked me to tell her again about the book I was writing.

"It's about an unusual friendship between two women, one in the middle and one at the end of her life."

"I don't like the reference to 'at the end of her life,'" Adele contested. Then it was as if reality had just set in. "Of course, I guess that's where I'm at. I'm closer to the end than I am to the middle. And if you can look back on your life with some satisfaction, you're lucky. I have no regrets. I say that sincerely."

"You're lucky to be able to say that," I said. I held Adele's arm tight. It felt good to be able to help her. In that instant, having to look back still seemed a long way away. I was young and the privileged one. We walked to the dining room menu board to see what was for dinner, and then we made fun of the food and laughed. We were friends again. This was the perfect visit.

I walked Adele back to her room, and I was ready to kiss her good-bye when she stopped in her doorway as if she had already forgotten I didn't have all the time in the world today to stand there and talk like she did.

"I got a call today." Adele's voice got very slow. "My sister died."

"Muriel?" I was as stunned as if I was talking about someone whose sister was forty, not eighty-five.

"Yes. She died yesterday in the hospital in New Jersey. Because of her heart."

"Oh, my God, Adele, I'm so sorry. Have you spoken with your niece yet? Do you want me to take you to the phone so you can call her?"

"I don't know," Adele said. "How do you console a person? Sometimes what we say just seems to make it worse."

I reached out and hugged Adele, and I couldn't let her go. Adele held me back tight. She was my father a year earlier when his last surviving sister died. She was me one day in the future left without one of my brothers. But now I stroked Adele's head as if she were my child.

"They're going to bury Muriel Sunday or Monday in the cemetery where I'll be buried. Now it will just be the space between her and my husband waiting for my body." Adele softly laid out this truth.

This was where I didn't know if it was still appropriate to hold Adele or if I should fall at her feet out of reverence to her serenity. What she had already seen I couldn't yet possibly know.

"Yup," Adele said. "Such is life. I guess I won't be going to my sister's funeral. I don't know. Should I fly all the way across the country and back for one day? No. It's too expensive." Adele straightened her blouse. "It wouldn't be practical." Adele backed into her room. It was dark in there and the curtains were drawn. "When might I see you again?"

"Tomorrow," I said. "I know you can't go to the funeral, but will you come to my house? I'm going to have a little party for my birthday. I want very much for you to be there."

"And meet your friends?"

"Yup. And let my other friends meet you."

A big smile came over Adele's face. "Yes, I'd like to meet your friends. Yes, I'd like to."

AM I OLD YET?

I woke up on my birthday feeling happy. It was a gorgeous California morning, and the birds were singing. I was forty-five and after all these years I was still alive! Life was astounding. In a few hours I was going to have the first party I had had in years for some of my favorite people in the world. This would be a day of many firsts. I was excited and filled with energy until I walked into the bathroom and looked in the mirror. Overnight the skin under my eyebrows had slid even closer toward my eyes. I panicked.

I had thought by adopting Adele I might get over my fears of aging, but here I was a year and a half later and it hadn't gotten better. My fears seemed to come less often, but they were worse because now I knew better. I knew without a doubt that there were no secret joys to be uncovered about getting old. I was not going to escape some of the deadliness of old age unless I was unlucky enough to die first. Maybe I could just have some fun.

Bob called to ask what he could do to help me that day.

"Nothing," I said. "Unless you can stop me from getting any older."

"The best I can do is promise that I'll always be three years older than you." Bob laughed.

"I'll take it," I said. My heart was pounding, while in my head I was trying to do the math on how many more lucid years Bob and I could have left together. Then I headed off to pick up Adele. Walking into the Chateau on my birthday was like walking into a cold shower. Nobody was around except a man who had fallen asleep over the pay phone.

"My sister was ten years younger than me, and she already died." Adele shook her head when I came to the door. Adele was wearing her dress shoes and her special frog brooch. I wanted to cry because she was so sweet and brave to make an effort to look pretty for a party when her sister's funeral was about to begin three thousand miles away.

"Do you think it ever happens that a person could be so lucky as to go to sleep one night and then just never wake up again?"

"Of course!" I said.

"Really?" For a moment Adele's voice seemed filled with possibility. "I wonder how I got to be the last person in my family to be alive. What will be will be. They say I'm going to start forgetting. They say that's what's coming next."

"Well, what's coming first is we'll be going to my house. Remember?"

"Oh, yes." Adele stepped back. "Is that today? I was thinking it's very nice that you invited me, but I don't want to ruin your party."

"What are you talking about?" I held Adele's hand. "You would never ruin the party. But if you're feeling too sad to be around a lot of new people, I understand."

"No, that's not it." Adele got very quiet. "But are you serving food? Because if you're eating, everyone will be looking at me to watch and see 'How does she eat?' and whatever, and I would feel uncomfortable being a big curiosity. After all, let's face it, I'm sure I will be the only person at the party who is blind."

I assured Adele that my friends all knew she was blind so it wouldn't be a mystery and that these were the kind of people who cared too much about their own food to be critical of how someone else ate theirs.

"If you want to come back here for your supper, I'll bring you back before we eat. You just tell me. I'll take you whenever you want. But please come. Everyone is just looking forward to meeting you."

Adele smiled. "Will your friend be there?"

"Bob? Yes, he'll be there."

Adele felt her way to the closet to get her sweater. "Good," she said. "Does he have a nice pension?"

When I pulled into my driveway, Eva and Richard and Cynthia and Dave and David and Mary Pat and Barb and Ray were already waiting out on the patio. They all watched how Adele got out of the car. I had gotten very used to walking with Adele and being her eyes. It was good to be able to help somebody, and I felt proud. I knew this was going to be the first time any of my friends had ever partied with someone who was almost ninety-five.

Everyone shook Adele's hand. My brother, Dan, and his wife, Marci, and my two young nieces, Katy and Kiya, drove in from Ojai. The girls seemed intrigued to meet Adele and not frightened when she touched them hello. Ray started up the barbecue, and Jenny called from her car phone. She had gotten tied up in an emergency meeting, but she would still be here. Then Bob walked in. He had flowers for me and he looked adorable. He was the only blue-collar guy there. He walked right up to Adele.

"Adele, this is Bob," I said, taking her hand so she could feel his.

"Hi, Adele," Bob said. He kissed her cheek.

"You have a beard!" Adele pulled back. "I don't like that."

Bob leaned forward and then he kissed Adele on the lips. "Is that better?" he asked.

"Much," Adele said, completely startled.

I laughed. That was the coolest thing I ever saw a man do in my life.

I took Adele's arm, and we walked together around my house.

"Don't you think it's exciting that Leah is writing a book about your friendship?" Barb asked Adele. "She's never written a book about me, and I've been her friend for twenty years!"

"Well, yes," Adele said. "Of course, I've been a reader my whole life. What's the title of that book again?"

"Am I Old Yet?" Barb said.

"Oh, dear." Adele laughed for a second. Then she got indignant. "I'm not old!"

"I'm not saying you are," I said. "I know you're not old!"

"Besides, old is just in time. I don't feel old in here." Adele pointed to her heart.

"The title is about me," I said. "Don't worry. I'm the one with the question."

"Well, if it makes you feel any better, you don't look old to me." Adele smiled.

Everybody cracked up. I laughed, too. Adele was a hit. I was delighted.

"You can be proud of having accumulated these friends." Adele squeezed my hand. "Of course, they could never improve on a friend like you, and you can tell them I said so. Believe me. You can know people from beginning to end but there's nothing there."

I looked at all these people and I felt peace. There was so much there. If I was lucky, there would be so much more to come. Today was the youngest day of the rest of my life, and I felt younger than I had in a decade. I knew it didn't make sense, but I was getting the picture that nothing about aging had ever made any sense. Maybe the beauty of getting older was knowing it probably never would. Somebody had just made a really big mistake. Perhaps one big, aggressive ad campaign could wipe the real problem of old age out forever—"Old is gold." Who knows what I might still see in my lifetime?

I watched Adele let Bob fix her a plate, and then he explained all the different foods he put on it. Smokey Robinson was on the radio, but nobody felt they had to turn it down because there was an old person around. Everyone ate. It was as natural as it always was. Adele was one of us.

"Delicious," Adele said. I could tell she was smiling right at me.

Then finally I knew. No matter how old a person is, if she has love in her life, there is only one age—alive.

SOURCES:
VOLUNTEERING TO BE
A FRIEND

ARE YOU INTERESTED IN VOLUNTEERING TO BE A FRIEND TO AN ELDER PERSON IN NEED?

Here are some sources for connecting with these people.

LOCAL

* Most counties have a *volunteer center* that acts as a clearinghouse for local charities and nonprofits that support elders in need. If you look in the Yellow Pages of your phone book under *Social Services Organizations,* you will find a listing for your volunteer center there. Or for more information on the volunteer center nearest you, call the National Volunteer Hotline at 1-800 CARE-123.

* You can also look in your local phone book directory in the Government Pages for your county's federally mandated *area agency on aging* for information about volunteer outreach programs and services as well as the *health and human services* division.

* Your local *Jewish community center* or *Jewish family and children's services* will, without fail, offer opportunities to be of service. Programs vary throughout the country. Two of these programs are the Senior Companionship Program (one-on-one visits, usually for one hour or more a week, with a year's commitment) and Stepping Out, which matches teens with seniors for weekly walks and other holiday visits. You do not have to be Jewish to volunteer here. These programs welcome people of all religions and

faiths. Check your local telephone directory or call the *Association of Jewish Family and Children's Agencies* at 1-800-634-7346. E-mail *AJFCA@aol.com.*

* Across America *universities, colleges, and junior colleges* often sponsor thriving volunteer or community services departments. Many offer the *adopt a grandparent* program which teams students with seniors for regular visits, often to nursing homes. Contact your nearest university, college, junior college, or institute of higher learning for further information.

NATIONAL AND INTERNATIONAL

* *Little Brothers—Friends of the Elderly.* For men and women, this is a nonprofit nonsectarian international organization. It was founded in Paris after World War II and helps those primarily still living in their own homes with little or no contact with family or friends and few financial resources. The national office is located at 954 West Washington Boulevard, Chicago, IL 60607. Phone: 312-829-3055. Other headquarters are in Boston, Cincinnati, Minneapolis/St. Paul, Philadelphia, San Francisco, and Houghton County, Michigan. Little Brothers also has offices in Canada, France, Germany, Ireland, Mexico, Morocco, and Spain. Their twenty-four-hour toll-free number is 888-805-1875. Or you can find them at *www.littlebrothers.org* on the Web.

* *Adopt a Native Elder* is a nonreligious, nonpolitical private charity that helps support Native American elders living on Navajo reser-

vations in northern New Mexico and southern Utah. Prospective volunteers are matched with an elder and may donate care parcels including food, clothing, or yarn (for Navajo rug weaving). Personal contact is limited. For more information contact Adopt a Native Elder, P.O. Box 3401, Park City, Utah 84060. Their phone number is 435-649-0535. You can also find them at *www.anelder.org* or E-mail them at mail@anelder.org.

Acknowledgments

I would not have been able to write this book without the love and support of so many people to whom I am eternally grateful.

I thank my friend and agent, Patti Breitman, who encouraged, nurtured, and patiently guided me to write a book for grown-ups. Without her brilliance, I wouldn't have written a page. Patti was also the first person I know who visited the elderly and planted the seed in me to do the same many years ago.

I thank Laura Yorke, my editor, for believing in this project from the beginning and for shaping its vision with her impeccable smarts, insight, and class. I thank Lara Asher for her additional editorial guidance and for consistently being upbeat, kind-hearted, and a total pro.

I am grateful to all of my supportive friends, including, for starters, a few who are also writers and shared their talents with me. First and foremost, Barbara Linkevitch, who listened to every single word day by day and who shared her expertise and time. I thank also David (Davy H.) Hoffman, Cynthia Emmets (spiritual dentist), and Elissa Van Poznak for researching the ways and means for befriending the elderly, which can be found in this book.

I thank Cheryl Kain for letting me read my "stories" to her over the phone every night before she went to sleep. "Good night, Cheryl."

I give so many thanks to the one and only Sally Perry and my office partners, Shoobuck and Dakota Perry. Brian Campbell, D.C., for saving my body and my computer. Mary Fitzpatrick, Tom Wraith, Betsy Baiker, Brenda Wilson, Jennifer Tash, Lisa Sonne, Bird and Tim Smith, Eva and Richard Andry, Frank Drendel, Annie Brody, Zelie Woodley, Robin Weisman, and Jill Champtaloup for being for me and behind me. I thank Arcona Devan for being the goddess and genius of beauty and youth, and the author, Knut Hamsun, for being my perpetual teacher. I thank Marilyn Gross for bringing Adele and me together.

I thank my father, the memory of my mother, Bill, Libby, Dan, Marci, Katy, and Kiya, without whom I would be lost.

I thank Bob Young, who literally walked with me every step of the way through this writing.

And finally, and most completely, I thank my most extraordinary friend Adele, who helped me get young and grow up a little before I got too old.

About the Author

LEAH KOMAIKO is the author of eighteen popular picture books and novels for kids, including the bestselling *Annie Bananie, Earl's Too Cool for Me,* and *I Like the Music.* She was commissioned by Liz Claiborne, Inc., to collaborate with twenty kids on a book about working mothers, which Maya Angelou called "sweet genius" and Claiborne published and distributed as a cause-related marketing campaign. Additionally, Komaiko's work has been featured in cause-related marketing campaigns for McDonald's and Hughes Aircraft. She has written multimedia projects for Disney and DreamWorks. Her work has been featured and reviewed on television and in dozens of magazines and newspapers. She has been a guest speaker in schools across the country as well as at numerous conventions and conferences. She lives in Los Angeles, California.